E

"This book will help you realize why managing tension by embracing Both/And thinking is the one skill every leader needs to succeed."

DONALD MILLER, CEO, STORYBRAND

"Why settle for one value when you can have two? Why settle for a limited point of view when you can expand your thinking and embrace the big picture? For us, leadership success is all about Both/And thinking!"

COLIN MCALLISTER AND JUSTIN RYAN, HGTV AND BBC TELEVISION STARS, THE DESIGN DUO

"I know Tim to be a successful and soulful leader who not only embraces tension, but effectively leverages it to grow results and relationships. His lived experience of leading with AND has been nothing short of transformative to the individuals and organizations he has worked alongside, myself included. *Lead with AND* is an invitation to bring your whole self to the leadership table, and to make a significant and sustained impact. I hope you accept it and experience the joy of the journey that is possible with AND!"

ALLISON ALLEY, PRESIDENT AND CEO, COMPASSION CANADA

"The desire to make the world a better place is not reserved for leaders. But if you choose to be a leader, it is essential for you to help the people you are privileged to serve experience that reality. It is hard work and can lead you to experience burnout or loss of purpose/passion.

"What makes this book exceptional and essential for all leaders is that this author is a leader, has made the world a better place, and knows a new way of thinking that helps every reader achieve that reality without burnout, exhaustion, and discouragement."

BONNIE WESORICK, RN, MSN, DPNAP, FAAN, HEALTHCARE VISIONARY

"Tim Arnold helps leaders get their teams out of draining, polarizing conflict. Leaders make an exponential impact on teams when they unlock clarity that helps people move forward together. *Lead with AND* resonates because it's practical, lasting, and works."

KELLY COWAN, ORGANIZATIONAL CHANGE CONSULTANT, ALLSTATE INSURANCE COMPANY OF CANADA

"Tim Arnold has a wonderful ability to take the concepts of polarity, paradox, and dilemma and make them applicable in meaningful ways. He has a knack for helping leaders recognize when they are dealing with problems that can't be solved—and wisdom in how he guides them to leverage these tensions so they can succeed."

CHANDRA IRVIN, EXECUTIVE DIRECTOR OF THE CENTER FOR PEACE AND SPIRITUAL RENEWAL, SPALDING UNIVERSITY

"In a culture increasingly characterized by binary thinking and the polarization of beliefs, many of us find ourselves struggling to understand, let alone constructively communicate with, the people on the other side of the divide—whatever that particular divide may be.

"Not many have the courage, and fewer still the insight, to offer workable 'bridges' that are practical enough to help us move forward when we get stuck organizationally, and still have the philosophical scope to offer the hope of healing for our deep societal wounds. With *Lead with AND*, Tim Arnold serves up all of that and more.

"No mere theoretician, his ideas and approaches have been tested in real-world settings where lives hang in the balance. Whether you see yourself as a line worker, visionary, or executive, this book will help you understand and address the obstacles that impede your progress and growth."

GREG PAUL, AUTHOR OF *THE TWENTY-PIECE SHUFFLE,* FOUNDER OF SANCTUARY MINISTRIES OF TORONTO

"In a world full of polarity, Tim Arnold and his brilliant approach to leveraging healthy tension helps us unravel the complexity of our leadership demands and find comfort in balancing competing ideas and concepts. This book couldn't have come at a better time!"

MELISSA MARTENS, LEAD, GLOBAL LEADERSHIP AND DIGITAL LEARNING, OMERS

"Tim Arnold has a wonderful gift for simplifying AND thinking without being simplistic. His many years of experience, deep compassion, and commitment to lifelong learning have all helped. A profound and practical book."

BARRY JOHNSON, FOUNDING PARTNER, POLARITY PARTNERSHIPS

"*Lead with AND* had a way of simultaneously inspiring and challenging me as a leader. Tim Arnold has written a book that's full of understanding and compassion towards the complexity of leadership, and provides incredibly practical tips and support for a myriad of challenges leaders face. He's not sugar-coating the challenges, but shares from his own insight and experience, and reminds you that you're not alone."

CHRISTA HESSELINK, FOUNDER AND CREATOR, SOULPLAY

"I've watched Tim Arnold teach the ideas found in this book to hundreds of colleagues over the last five years, and the feedback I consistently receive is some version of 'Wow, these tools have changed my life for the better.' Tim challenges his readers to grow into healthier versions of themselves. There's no question that I am a more empowered and effective leader because of AND thinking."

KATE MASSON, COMMUNITY MANAGER, THE IAN MARTIN GROUP

"If you are a leader of a team in any setting, then this book is the essential guide to achieving the results you want and enjoying the journey. Building on the principles in Tim's first book, *The Power of Healthy Tension*, this book provides a guide for managing the six tensions that we face every day as leaders. By learning to manage these tensions and shift our thinking from Either/Or to Both/And, we can unlock the potential in ourselves and the teams we lead.

"I find myself applying the concepts in *Lead with AND* in both my personal and professional life, and the book thoroughly deserves its place on my 'leadership 101' bookshelf alongside Kim Scott's *Radical Candor* and Patrick Lencioni's *The Ideal Team Player*."

IAN YATES, DIRECTOR, ENTERPRISE SCIENCE AND INNOVATIVE PARTNERSHIPS, THERMO FISHER SCIENTIFIC

"My team and I were feeling burnt out, exhausted, and very disconnected. Working through the chapters of *Lead with AND* gave us the words to have conversation around topics we were struggling to articulate in both our personal and professional lives. *Lead with AND* offers easy-to-learn, actionable takeaways that are timely and relevant. I highly recommend this book!"

JOANNE GEORGE, NATIONAL WHOLESALE MANAGER, PARKLAND CORPORATION

"Just when I thought our world couldn't get any more divided, it seems people have found a way to become even more polarized. This has made the past season the most challenging ever for leaders, never mind for life. Thankfully, Tim Arnold has provided a next-level gift in *Lead with AND* to help us navigate the most delicate and difficult times of our generation.

"There are countless places you can look to be told that you ought to stimulate more unity. And there are limitless books, podcasts, and webinars that teach that leaders should manage change well.

"What separates Tim and his writings from these is that he actually teaches us how. He provides a practical framework, real-life stories, and everyday examples to help us live and lead effectively in precarious times.

"The pace of life these days and the rate at which things change may tempt you to believe you don't have time to read yet another book. But this isn't just another book; it's a practical guide to help you navigate the very changes and challenges you face every day in life and leadership."

JEFF LOCKYER, LEAD PASTOR, SOUTHRIDGE COMMUNITY CHURCH

"Learning how to lead with AND has built resilience within our leaders and is inspiring them to move forward with confidence."

IDA THOMAS, VICE PRESIDENT, PEOPLE AND CULTURE, YMCA CANADA

"As a people leader, I am regularly faced with conflicting decisions that have a direct impact on my leadership. Tim effectively highlights, through relatable examples and engaging interviews, the ability to lean into these polarities across the most relevant tensions of today's leaders. He leaves the reader with the courage to embrace the AND to take their leadership to the next level. A must read for any leader!"

JENNIFER LINDLEY, MANAGER, LEARNING AND ORGANIZATIONAL DEVELOPMENT, ALECTRA UTILITIES

"In our rapidly growing medical device business, no leadership concept has been as 'sticky' and impactful as leading with AND. It has become reflex to use this one word to avoid polarization and drive to solution-based thinking in our teams. As a result, we stay focused on what matters: delivering technologies that improve the lives of patients around the world. This [book] has become my go-to leadership toolbox!"

ROBERT HARRISON, DIRECTOR OF R&D, CARDIOLOGY, BAYLIS MEDICAL COMPANY

LEAD
WITH
AND

The Secret to Resilience and
Results in a Polarized World

TIM ARNOLD

To Becky,
my teammate in all of life's adventures.
I married up!

CONTENTS

FOREWORD

By Donald Miller

One of the reasons leaders stop growing and succeeding is because they get tired of managing tension. Managing tension, though, does not have to be draining. As leaders, our primary job is to solve problems and manage tension, and our ability to do so is the only reason people give us more responsibilities. Most leaders have never been taught a healthy way to manage tension. That's why I think this book is so important.

Being able to hold things in tension is the single most important skill we can develop to succeed in nearly any area of life. Leaders need to understand that tension isn't bad, and it's always going to happen. Beyond that, they need to realize if they have the skills and courage to manage tension well, and stop expecting it to go away, they will make it very, very far personally and professionally.

This book will help you realize that managing tension by embracing Both/And thinking is the whole job!

———

Donald Miller is the author of best-selling books, including Building a StoryBrand *and* Blue Like Jazz. *He is also the CEO of Business Made Simple, an online platform that teaches business professionals everything they need to know to grow a business and enhance their personal value on the open market.*

INTRODUCTION

The Big Idea

B y learning to lead with AND, you will break through to a new level of resilience and results. For organizations that are struggling due to complexity and chronic issues, you will provide clarity and lead sustainable change. For teams and relationships that are divided and polarized, you will provide alignment and connection. For individuals who are stuck due to overdone black-or-white thinking, you will provide confidence to navigate the grey.

Leaders are responsible to move things forward and driven to make a difference. Sadly, I have witnessed too many high-potential leaders throw in the towel because they believed the cost of leadership was too high. I have also worked beside a long list of leaders who didn't give up, but the uphill battle required to lead against broken systems, impossible demands, and unreasonable people made them bitter and jaded.

Your work is important, and right now, the world needs your leadership more than ever!

I wrote this book to provide leaders with the one skill every leader needs to succeed: a proven way to successfully stay in the game and enjoy the adventure. I wrote this book because your work is important, and right now, the world needs your leadership more than ever!

In 2017, I published *The Power of Healthy Tension,* inviting readers to move beyond the limitations of overdone Either/Or thinking and instead embrace the power of Both/And thinking.

That book was deliberately conceptual and looked at things from a high level.

This book explores the same powerful phenomenon, but at a practical level, with ideas you can immediately put into action.

By the end of this book, you will know how to successfully 1. understand, 2. assess, and 3. leverage the following six leadership tensions:

- Leadership Tension #1: Being Optimistic AND Realistic
- Leadership Tension #2: Embracing Change AND Preserving Stability
- Leadership Tension #3: Being Profit Focused AND Purpose Driven
- Leadership Tension #4: Having Expectations AND Extending Grace
- Leadership Tension #5: Caring for Others AND Caring for Yourself
- Leadership Tension #6: Building Confidence AND Remaining Humble

The Breakdown

CHAPTER 1
Dead End On The Road Less Travelled

As a leader, you're committed to making a difference, leaving a mark, and changing the world for the better. The problem is you continue to find yourself stuck in complex situations with chronic issues and polarizing demands. Is the only option to settle for a watered-down version of your vision and values, or worse, to throw in the towel altogether? What if the secret to resilience, results, and peace of mind is to embrace the very thing that you are currently avoiding?

CHAPTER 2

Tension Is Not A Bad Word

Whether we realize it or not, holding things in tension is something most of us avoid. Instead, the temptation is to pick a side, go full throttle in one direction, and double down on one point of view. However, when we avoid the tension between certain conflicting values, we inevitably end up fighting a lose-lose battle that leads to division, bitterness, and burnout. But how do you know whether you're dealing with a problem to solve or a tension to manage? And what does it take to stop avoiding tension and start leveraging it instead?

CHAPTER 3

The Foundations Of Resilience (Optimism AND Realism)

You set out to make a difference, leave a mark, and change the world. However, it's beginning to feel like you're living in a world of compromise, trade-offs, and settling for *just OK*. You don't want to sell out or lose your grit and resolve, but you also need to sleep at night and have a life. After all, the needs of others will always be there. How can you continue to be a visionary and idealist while finding peace when facing the reality of the current situation?

Featuring an interview with Allison Alley, President and CEO, Compassion Canada.

CHAPTER 4

Outsmarting Change (Change AND Stability)

It seems that the reward for success is more work. Now that your name and reputation are getting established, there are more opportunities coming your way than ever before: potential partnerships, new ideas for products or services, support for growth and expansion, and so on. The question is, how much is too much? How do you know when the benefits of change are coming at the expense of your mission? How can you leverage new opportunities without losing your core values and proven practices?

Featuring an interview with Tim Schurrer, COO, StoryBrand.

CHAPTER 5

Big Dreams Versus The Bottom Line (Profit AND Purpose)

You are conditioned to accept the fact that some people (and organizations) are all about making money—the 1%, the greedy, and the privileged—while others are all about making a difference—servant leaders, humanitarians, and charities. What if the most powerful strategy for long-term impact is to pursue both? What if profit *and* purpose are the best formula to change the world?

Featuring an interview with Colin McAllister and Justin Ryan, HGTV and BBC Television Stars, The Design Duo.

CHAPTER 6

The High-Performance Paradox (Expectations AND Grace)

You know that goals and objectives motivate you toward focus and high performance. You also know that, as a leader, it's your job to see and call out the best in others. At the same time, non-stop high expectations often lead to resentment, stress, and burnout. It's also true that everyone you work with is fighting a battle you know nothing about. How do you stay driven toward goals and excellence while still holding on to empathy and acceptance for yourself and others?

Featuring an interview with Chandra Irvin, Executive Director of the Center for Peace and Spiritual Renewal, Spalding University.

CHAPTER 7

All In But Burnt Out (Self AND Others)

When looking beneath the surface of some of the most incredible difference-makers in history, you'll often find family breakdowns, health issues, depression, and burnout. The sad reality is that making a difference often comes at a high personal cost. Is there a way to lay down your life and have a life? Is there a secret to caring for others while not neglecting yourself in the process?

Featuring an interview with Jason Russell, Filmmaker and Activist, Co-founder of Invisible Children, Inc.

CHAPTER 8

Do I Have What It Takes? (Confidence AND Humility)

On many levels, you realize you've grown in your leadership and have come a long way in figuring out how to make a difference. Yet, rarely a day goes by when you're not reminded of how little you know and how far you have to go. You feel responsible to speak out, teach others, and leverage your voice. Yet, you know that you have more questions than answers. Is it possible to stand firmly in confidence while being grounded in humility at the same time?

Featuring an interview with Marnie McBean, Three-time Olympic Gold Medallist.

CHAPTER 9

"Uncommon" Sense Leadership

We live in a polarized world. Every day we see an ever-increasing division between people, politics, and perspectives. Liberal versus conservative. Environment versus economy. Unions versus management. Black Lives Matter versus All Lives Matter. We desperately need leaders who can build bridges that unify instead of walls that divide. What does it take to move beyond the common lose-lose scenario and guide divided people toward a higher purpose?

Featuring an interview with Greg Paul, Author of The Twenty-Piece Shuffle, *Founder of Sanctuary Ministries of Toronto*

CHAPTER 10

How To Stay In The Game (And Enjoy The Adventure)

There is hope. You've read inspiring examples of change-makers, communities, and companies that have successfully blazed a trail down the path less travelled. You've seen that it is possible to make a difference and hold onto principles and peace of mind. Now it's your turn! Be the leader who finally has the confidence and courage to break through to a new level of resilience and results and pave a way for others to do the same.

Featuring an interview with Bonnie Wesorick, RN, MSN, DPNAP, FAAN, Healthcare Visionary

The Author

There are a few things you should know about me to fully understand and appreciate this book. Although I had a solid upbringing with two loving parents, I was raised to only see the world through a black-or-white lens. Tied to religious fundamentalism and what was referred to in our house as "simple common sense," things were either right or wrong, correct or incorrect, good or evil.

This didn't work out too well for me as I moved into the complexity of adulthood and found that my overdone Either/Or approach to life resulted in significant struggles both at work and at home. In my late 20s, I was introduced to the idea of holding values in tension and taking an AND approach to life, and everything changed. I started to breakthrough to new levels of personal and professional success.

My professional career has been quite eclectic. After spending 10 years running a team-building business that served hundreds of companies each year, I did a 180 and sold the company to take on the role of director for a 40-bed homeless shelter. Over the next decade, I led a team that continually expanded our homelessness programs and services, and launched a social enterprise that provided opportunities for our friends who were transitioning from the streets to gain meaningful employment.

Finally, after moving from a staff position to a volunteer role at the homeless shelter, I launched Leaders for Leaders, a leadership development company that is committed to *both* profit *and* purpose.

My ever-changing career has given me the rare opportunity to help leaders, ranging from Nobel Peace Prize winners to Fortune 500 CEOs, successfully navigate the path to resilience and results. It has also had me working with professionals on

Wall Street *and* supporting the poor and excluded under bridges and in alleyways. I will do my best to integrate all this experience and perspective into the chapters you are about to read.

Now for the best part. Every day, I get to come home to three of the most amazing people in the world: my wife, Becky, and our two children, Declan and Avryl. Their unconditional love and the challenges we face together have provided me with some of the most powerful learning and insight. Expect to hear more about them as well!

The Content

My primary focus in writing this book was providing clarity around Step One (Understanding) and Step Two (Assessing) for each of the six leadership tensions. For Step Three (Leveraging), instead of trying to recreate the wheel, I have provided you with proven models, tools, and strategies from brilliant authors and thought leaders. Over the years as I've learned how to tap into healthy tension, these are the same tools that I've found to be a powerful catalyst in sustaining positive change. By curating them and putting them all together in this book, I hope to provide you with a fantastic "best of" in leadership development.

The Experts

In each of the six chapters that focus on a key leadership tension (Chapters 3 through 8), you will find a section called AND Leadership in Action. These contain insights from interviews that I conducted with leaders from around the world—each showing mastery in leveraging the specific tension of that chapter. The goal of these interviews is to provide you with practical and actionable things you can do to take advantage of each tension, while identifying red flags that may indicate that the tension is being mismanaged.

As I was writing the outline for the book and narrowed down my list of leadership tensions, I made a wish list of my ideal people to interview. I knew that it was a long shot, but I reached out to each person to see if they would be interested in helping out with this book and, to my surprise, every single one of them said yes.

Prepare to hear from incredible women and men from a wide variety of leadership roles. From acclaimed CEOs and Olympic athletes to world-renowned human rights activists and celebrity lifestyle gurus, all the interviewees blew me away with their insight and wisdom, and I am excited for you to benefit from what they had to say as well.

The Pandemic

I started pulling together the big ideas of this book throughout 2019, and then, in February of 2020, I completed the formal outline with a commitment to have the manuscript completed by the fall of that year. But then this little thing called COVID-19 happened.

By the end of March 2020, I was in survival mode with my business as 75% of our bookings were cancelled or postponed. My focus on writing this book had to shift as pivoting the business to navigate the pandemic needed all my attention. Thankfully, our business ended up thriving through the pandemic, and by the end of 2020, we'd had our most successful year by far.

Interestingly, surviving and ultimately thriving through the pandemic forced me to put all of the concepts of this book to the test. Was the ability to manage key tensions truly the one leadership skill needed to succeed? Were the key leadership tensions actually the make-it-or-break-it ones to be managed in order to achieve resilience and results?

Thankfully, the answer was yes. I don't know if our business would have survived the pandemic if we had not had the ability to lead with AND. I found that in incredibly challenging times, I was proud of our level of resilience and pleased with the results we experienced. Much of this was due to our ability to navigate tension in a healthy way.

I mention COVID-19 many times throughout the following chapters as it was such a dominant reality in my life as I was writing the book. When you see the words "COVID-19," you can simply substitute any challenge or force beyond your control and the content will instantly become timely and relevant for you.

That's it! That's all you need to know to fully engage with the chapters you are about to read. Are you ready to learn the one skill every leader needs to succeed? Here we go!

Lead with AND

An approach to leadership that moves beyond divisive Either/Or thinking and instead embraces Both/And thinking

The secret to both *resilience* and *results*

FREE RESOURCE

To thank you for purchasing this book, I want to provide you with a free resource that will allow you to create a personal action plan around key concepts and big ideas.

Simply visit www.LeadWithAnd.com and download the Personal Action Plan. This digital journal includes chapter summaries, tension maps, and assessment grids, as well as space for you to create a plan you can immediately put into action.

WWW.LEADWITHAND.COM

CHAPTER 1

DEAD END ON THE ROAD LESS TRAVELLED

*"Two roads diverged in a wood and I—I took the one
less traveled by, and that has made all the difference."*

ROBERT FROST

L eadership is a fascinating thing. A leader has the power
to make the world a better place and the power to divide
and destroy. It's a title that many people aspire to hold, yet it's
a responsibility that often results in stress, disappointment, and
relationship breakdown.

It is important to start by defining the word "leader"; however, I've been working in the leadership development world
long enough to know that this is a controversial thing to do.
What a leader is (and isn't) has inspired centuries of debate and
disagreement.

So, know that this isn't the definition of leadership, it is simply *my* definition of leadership, one that has developed through
years of studying leadership, working with leaders, and trying to
lead myself.

LEADER – *A person who is responsible to move things forward and driven to make a difference*

Responsible to Move Things Forward

Leaders are trailblazers. I think that most people assume this means moving *people* forward. They believe that to be a leader, you need to lead people as a boss, a manager, or a supervisor. And certainly, this is one example of leadership, but it is a limited perspective. I know many leaders who don't lead people, but instead, they move *projects* forward. They have a high level of responsibility on their shoulders and must deliver on make-it-or-break-it work assignments. They take ownership of projects that aren't for the faint of heart.

Based on these two perspectives, when I talk about leadership, know that I am talking about both people-leaders and project-leaders.

Driven to Make a Difference

Leaders are difference-makers. Most of the time, this is a good thing and comes from a healthy place. People-leaders are excited to play a role in helping the people they lead thrive. Project-leaders want to see the tasks they're working on move the organization forward or impact the world in a positive way. This kind of drive to make a difference is synonymous with healthy passion, motivation, and desire.

> *We may not all consider ourselves to be leaders, or aspire to have that title, but we all desire to make a difference.*

Unfortunately, the drive to make a difference can also come from an unhealthy, dysfunctional place. These leaders work hard to make a difference, but their primary motive is to establish a name and reputation or to earn rewards for themselves. This unhealthy drive to make a difference is synonymous with ego, pride, and selfish ambition.

I think if we're honest, our drive to lead can easily come from a bit of both places.

When it comes to this idea of being driven to make a difference, here's what I have learned to be true: Regardless of whether you see yourself as a leader or not, there is something inside all of us that longs for impact and significance. We all want to make a difference!

- **I saw this in the shelter.** Throughout the decade I spent directing a 40-bed homeless shelter, I would see this desire to make a difference lived out every single day in our incredible volunteers. Whether they were preparing meals, answering phones, or playing a game of cards with our residents, they faithfully came back week after week, hoping that the few hours they invested could provide someone with the support needed to get their life back on track.

- **I saw this as a corporate trainer.** Each year, I offer a six-month emerging leadership program for young professionals from across the world. Every time I launch a new cohort, I'm blown away by the determination of each participant to become a difference-maker. This drives them to understand and apply every concept we explore and excites them to know what we'll cover next. They are grateful for the opportunity they've been given to lead and are bursting with enthusiasm to make the world a better place.

- **I saw this in my neighbourhood.** When my mother-in-law, Austin, was diagnosed with stage-four cancer, friends and neighbours astonished us with their offers to help out. They dropped off meals, provided rides to appointments, cut the lawn, and offered encouraging words.

  On what we assumed would be Austin's final birthday, we wanted to celebrate, but due to COVID-19 restrictions, we had to limit our gatherings and be socially distant. Despite these setbacks, I watched the community brainstorm a "birthday parade" that would travel past her house with socially distant birthday wishes. The parade ended up spanning as far as the eye could see and included everyone from close friends and family to local politicians and the fire department (with full-on lights and sirens).

- **I've experienced this personally.** This might seem a bit silly of an example, but every time I watch the reality TV show, Extreme Home Makeover, I'm a weepy mess by the end of the episode. Without fail, the moment the host and volunteers yell out at the top of their lungs, "MOVE THAT BUS!," I fall apart.

There's something about seeing an extreme example of difference-making that cuts right to the heart.

And it's not just reality TV. There is rarely a day that goes by that I'm not thinking about the impact (or lack thereof) I'm making in the world. Am I doing enough? As someone born with great privilege and who has access to endless opportunity, am I leveraging all of this to make a positive difference in the world?

We may not all consider ourselves to be leaders, or aspire to have that title, but we *all* desire to make a difference.

The Fine Print

You've listened to the voice inside you daring you to lead. You've tapped into the courage required to take the road less travelled and now have people looking to you for direction and development, or you have projects with incredibly high stakes resting on your shoulders. You've chosen adventure and impact over caution and comfort.

So why are you feeling more frustrated than you've ever been? Why does it seem that the systems you are working within are broken beyond repair? Why are the people you're working for (and sometimes with) so unreasonable and irrational? Why are you constantly dealing with expectations that are impossible to deliver on?

Could it be that when you signed up for the road less travelled, you forgot to read the fine print? Let's look at a few examples to illustrate what I mean. (Below are just the beginnings of these stories. You'll read the rest in Chapter 2. You'll also learn why all three stories are relevant to the idea of leading with AND. Stay tuned!)

A Company Catastrophe

My friend, Tim Masson, was 32 when he decided to take the road less travelled. For months, people were privately approaching him to see if he planned on taking over the family business due to his father's rapid decline from early Alzheimer's disease.

At the time, Tim was a software developer and didn't see himself as qualified or experienced enough to lead his family's recruiting business with hundreds of staff. However, after trying to think of many alternatives to the problem, he finally walked into the CFO's office and said, "I want the job."

> "I've always enjoyed challenging work and was totally loving my developer job at the time. When I thought back, however, I realized there was a time in my life that I had loved my work even more; it was in university when I led a volunteer organization each summer with a team of about 75 people. Everyone was having fun and passionately engaged in their work. We shared a common purpose, developed positive relationships, and worked hard to position each person into meaningful work.

> "This made me wonder if it might be possible to lead a business in a similar way. With this new leadership opportunity, I'd have a chance to influence hundreds, possibly thousands, of employees, clients, and partners in a positive direction, connecting them to meaningful, purpose-driven work. I knew this would probably be my biggest chance in life to make a difference."

Tim immediately went to work in pursuit of this vision. One of the first changes involved the company becoming a Certified B Corporation.[1] In a commitment to pursue both profit and purpose, this certification required the company to live up to the highest standards of verified social and environmental performance, public transparency, and legal accountability.

Tim also deconstructed and reconstructed roles and responsibilities. This meant moving away from a traditional hierarchy and becoming more of a flat, self-managed organization which gave *all* employees freedom and shared leadership.

Fast forward about two years. Tim is on the receiving end of yet another long-standing senior employee scornfully asking, "Are you willing to be the one on whose watch, after 60 years, the business fails so you can hold on to these *values* of yours?"

At that time, the business was close to bankruptcy. Tim was starting to deal with ongoing anxiety and panic attacks related to the poor health and unknown future of the company.

> "I had to decide whether it was worth it. Should I stick to my guns and push forward with my beliefs, even when the skeptics were constantly telling me (and everyone else in the company) that I was naïve and tearing things apart? I started to wonder if pursuing a vision and trying to make a difference could only come at the cost of my happiness and peace of mind."

A Political Disaster
Walter Sendzik could have chosen an easier road. Moving into his 40s, he had already founded, built, and sold a national wine magazine. He followed this up with becoming CEO of the Greater

Niagara Chamber of Commerce, building it into the largest business organization in Niagara and the third largest chamber in Ontario. He was also on a number of influential boards.

Walter was well positioned to continue to move up the corporate success ladder, but a voice in the back of his head kept telling him that he had an opportunity to use his talents and connections to make a difference in his own community. At the time, the mid-sized city of St. Catharines was in a bit of a rough place. Unemployment was rising, the downtown was struggling, and the younger generation was leaving for opportunities that only seemed to exist in bigger cities across the country.

> "I started to believe that as mayor, I could use my talents to turn things around. At the end of the day, I wanted to help build a city so vibrant that my kids would want to stay and establish their own families here."

Walter succeeded in being elected mayor and immediately got to work. He brought in private sector partners and various levels of government to support community projects and initiatives. As a strong advocate for local business, he engaged corporate leaders to assist in drafting a new strategic plan and economic development strategy that was quickly approved. Understanding how critical transportation was for business success and getting people to work, school, and services, he led the development of an intermunicipal transit service that would connect all of Niagara's communities.

The most unique and attention-grabbing thing Walter did, however, was to launch the Compassionate City initiative.[2] As a growing city, St. Catharines was not immune to challenges like poverty, addictions, and homelessness. Based on a conviction that the true wealth and well-being of a city could only be measured by the wealth and well-being of everyone, Walter's vision for the Compassionate City initiative was to inspire and challenge city residents to care about and reach out to the poor and marginalized. This included providing sensitivity training for city staff and Council, breaking down barriers to access city services and resources, and freeing up staff and budget for poverty reduction and affordable housing programs.

Unfortunately, the honeymoon phase didn't last long, and it seemed that no matter who you talked to, Walter was falling short of expectations. Business leaders were voicing their concerns (both privately and publicly) that he seemed more concerned about helping the "bums and crackheads" than he was about helping businesses grow and creating jobs. Leaders in the world of poverty reduction criticized him for not going far enough or fast enough in implementing real change, such as requiring city businesses to pay a living wage. They complained that the Compassionate City initiative was nothing more than a marketing effort.

It was starting to feel like a lose-lose situation. Was this as good as it gets in the life of a politician? Was giving up all the opportunity and freedom that he once enjoyed as an entrepreneur and CEO a naïve decision? Was laying it all on the line to make a real difference worth it?

A Migrant Worker Mess

In the 1960s, a labour shortage existed on Canadian farms, specifically on the tender fruit farms of Southern Ontario. The Canadian government launched a program aimed at fixing this problem by allowing Jamaican workers to come to Canada for up to eight months to assist on the farms. Today, this program brings more than 20,000 workers annually from Mexico and the Caribbean, helping out at over 1,600 farms and greenhouses.

Mary Ann Schlabach was 31 years old when the first Jamaican workers came to Niagara in 1966. She and her husband, Breland, owned a grocery store in the small town of Vineland, Ontario. The Caribbean men working on nearby farms would walk to her store to get their groceries. Because they were only paid bi-weekly or monthly, they often were short on cash. "We would keep a book to record their credits and tell them they could straighten up at the end of the month," she explained, adding that they never once went without payment.

As Mary Ann and her husband got to know their Caribbean neighbours, visit them at their farms, and learn about their families and communities, it became clear to her that she was meant to help them. "It was interesting," she said. "As a registered nurse, I was asked to move to Nigeria to work on an outreach there. Although I strongly considered going, something told me my mission was here at home."

She committed her life to finding ways to help overcome the isolation, stigmatization, and loneliness these men faced in Canada. However, it seemed that this would force her to choose sides.

When she looked at others who were reaching out to support the local Caribbean workers, they normally took an "anti-farmer" approach. As these men and women got to know the migrant workers, sometimes they would see living conditions on the farms that were unacceptable, notice working conditions that were unsafe, and hear stories of mistreatment. As a result, they would spread the word to friends, neighbours, and even the press that farmers were the "bad guys" in their exploitation of the local migrant workers.

Within a short amount of time, the divide was clear between farmers and people who were reaching out to the Caribbean workers. Farmers didn't trust these "activists" who should be minding their own business, and outreach workers believed that farmers were the perpetrators of injustice.

This posed a serious dilemma for Mary Ann. The local farmers were her friends and her customers. Beyond this, she herself was born and raised on a farm and knew of the hard work and sacrifices required of farming families to make a living and make a difference. If she listened to the inner voice telling her to take the road less travelled, did that mean she would have to sever her relationships and damage her reputation with the local farming community? Was the only way to make a difference to choose sides?

Is It Worth It?

If these stories are typical examples of what to expect as a leader, you have to ask yourself, "Is taking the road less travelled worth it?"

Does stepping up to new levels of responsibility and stress in the hopes of making a difference inevitably mean stepping into a life of resistance and frustration? Is it simply a leadership expectation to have to settle for a watered-down version of your vision and values? Is it impossible to make a positive impact in the world and still lead a normal life?

Here's the good news: *No! It doesn't have to be this way.*

In the following chapters, I am going to offer you a better option. The road less travelled doesn't lead to a dead end! You are about to discover how taking an AND approach to leadership will help you build resilience and deliver results.

But prepare yourself, because the secret I'm about to share with you will require you to embrace the very thing you are currently avoiding.

CHAPTER 2

TENSION IS NOT A BAD WORD

Learn to Embrace What Others Avoid

I n the year that this book is being written, leadership development is a $366 billion global industry, and over 1,500 books will
be published with the word "leadership" or "leader" in the title.
These books will add to the over 60,000 already available for pur-
chase on Amazon, all providing models and theories guaranteed
to equip you for leadership success.

With all this instruction and training, you would assume
that aspiring leaders would have all they need to thrive, that
there would be solutions to all the leadership challenges they
would face. Yet despite all these leadership solutions, when you
look around, it can be quite hard to find an example of great leadership in action:

- CEO salaries in major corporations continue to
  grow exponentially faster than average pay. In
  Canada where I live, the country's 100 highest-paid
  CEOs made 202 times more than the average
  working Canadian in 2019. You would assume that

this compensation is a just reward for exceptional leadership, but many of these CEOs rationalize that a large percentage of their employees make less than a living wage, fail to model diversity and inclusion in their workplaces, and find every way possible to avoid paying their fair share in taxes to help the country (and its people) thrive.

- The state of our democracies—at least in the western world—is in crisis. Elected "leaders" often feel little responsibility to be truthful. Instead, they tend to toe the party line no matter how helpful or hurtful it may be, tell their voters what they want to hear, and, by default, vilify the opposition and its values.

- Study after study shows that the rates of stress, anxiety, depression, and divorce often increase when a person is promoted in the workplace. This suggests that an increase in leadership responsibility often results in a decrease of personal wellness and a healthy home life.

If leaders have easy access to solutions for all the problems they face, why do they (and the people and organizations they lead) often struggle?

Why is this our current reality? If leaders have easy access to solutions for all the problems they face, why do they (and the people and organizations they lead) often struggle? Is it possible that despite all the models, theories, courses, books, and consultants, something is still missing?

What if I told you (and show you in the chapters to come) that the primary reason it's so hard to see great leadership in action is because leaders are mistakenly treating every challenge they face as a problem to solve using an Either/Or approach, when in reality, they are tensions to manage using Both/And thinking? What if the "uncommon" sense approach of learning to hold things in tension and taking an AND approach to leadership could provide you with a secret advantage as a leader, a clear path to *both* resilience *and* results?

The Problem with Problem Solving

When I'm speaking to large audiences, I often conduct a short but insightful activity. I tell the group that I'm going to show them a series of slides, each slide containing a word and a picture. All they have to do is either stay seated if they are against what's on the slide or stand up if they are for what's on the slide. Here are some of the words and pictures I commonly display:

- Pineapple on pizza
- Reality TV
- Cilantro
- Cats
- Crocs
- NASCAR

What's fascinating is that *every* time I do this activity, a few things inevitably happen:

1. People either stand up or sit down within a second of seeing the slide. There is little processing or

internal debate. They are clearly for or against what is on the slide.

2. As soon as people stand or sit, they immediately look around for others who share their opinion. This affirmation seems to provide them with a sense of confidence and relief. It's as if they have connected with a community of like-minded individuals.

3. Each side seems to share a light-hearted but real disdain for the other side's point of view. The people against cats are looking at one another shaking their heads in disgust. The people for Crocs (an often small but brazen group) look around at one another with a look of superiority.

Why does this happen? What is it within us that loves to jump to an opinion and then look to be affirmed in that opinion? Why do we sometimes assume that others who don't share our values and points of view just don't get it?

The reason is that about 99.9% of my audiences are overly fixated on problem solving, and chances are—you might have a problem with problem solving as well.

Problem solving requires an Either/Or approach. You either like pineapple on pizza or you don't. You either love spending your Sunday afternoon watching NASCAR or you think that watching cars going in circles for hours upon hours is incredibly silly and a complete waste of time.

Problem solving assumes that for every challenge you face, there is a right and a wrong answer. And if you are reading this book, no matter who you are, I guarantee you are a skilled problem solver. I know this because problem solving is something that you've been trained and rewarded for your entire life.

This all started before you could walk or talk. As soon as your parents brought you home from the hospital, they started teaching you that things were either safe or unsafe.

> Go here but don't go there. Touch this but don't touch
> that. Eat this but don't eat that.

This continued when you started attending school and were taught that there was either a correct or an incorrect answer for every question you would be tested on.

> Two plus two equals four.
> The Dominion of Canada began on July 1, 1867.
> Energy equals mass times the speed of light squared.

You also learned that if you could choose the correct answer, you might receive the coveted gold star on the top of your test paper. However, if you chose the incorrect answer, you would end up with the shameful red X instead.

Your development in problem solving progressed into your teenage years when your parents, schools, and community all started to have you focus more on values and morals.

> Be polite.
> Service before self.
> Leave things in better condition than you found them.

They wanted you to understand that the choices you make in life would dictate whether you became *either* a good *or* a bad person. It became clear that there were paths you could go down in life, and if you chose the right path, you could become a good and successful person; if you chose the wrong path, you could end up living a life of shame and failure.

So, by the time you were a young adult, whether you realized it or not, you were indoctrinated to believe that for every challenge you faced, if you could just choose the *right* answer, you would be safe, correct, and a good person. The world succeeded in developing you into an expert problem solver with highly tuned Either/Or thinking.

But don't get me wrong, this is a good thing! Your ability to solve problems is critical to your success in life and as a leader. Many challenges you face are in fact problems to solve and require Either/Or thinking. Some things are safe or unsafe, correct or incorrect, good or bad. And when you encounter these situations, the best thing you can do is to choose the right answer as efficiently and effectively as possible, solve the problem, and move on.

However, as I'm sure you've come to realize, sometimes life is more complicated than your default problem-solving approach allows for. For example:

> Should you be truthful *or* should you be tactful?
> Should you be optimistic *or* should you be realistic?
> Should you have high expectations *or* should you
> have high levels of grace?
> Should you manage costs *or* should you invest
> in quality?
> Should you care for others *or* should you care
> for yourself?

Should you be confident *or* should you be humble?
Should you be structured *or* should you be flexible?
Should you embrace change *or* should you
preserve stability?
Should you focus on work *or* should you focus
on home?

The answer to all of these questions is...YES!

And if you deal with any of the above challenges with an Either/Or, problem-solving approach, it will backfire. These are situations that require Both/And thinking. They require you to lead with AND.

Early into his first term as president, Barack Obama was interviewed by *Rolling Stone* magazine[1] and said this, "The issues that cross my desk are hard and complicated, and oftentimes involve the clash not of right and wrong, but of two rights. And you're having to balance and reconcile against competing values that are equally legitimate."

He was realizing what I'm sure you've come to realize: the more responsibility you take on as a leader, and the more you aim to make a difference in the world, the more you inevitably find yourself wrestling with complex issues that don't have easy answers, issues that other people either choose to ignore or create overly simplistic solutions to that just don't work long term.

Let's go back to the examples I shared in the previous chapter of aspiring difference-makers who were all dealing with significant dilemmas.

- **A Company Catastrophe** – As CEO, Tim began
  to realize that he was wrestling with the tension

of *either* embracing change *or* preserving stability. Was it possible for him to move forward with his vision requiring team and company disruption *and* hold onto the best practices and traditions that had served the company well for the last 60 years?

- **A Political Disaster** – As mayor, Walter realized that he was wrestling with the tension of maintaining *either* economic responsibility *or* social responsibility. Was it possible for him to invest in business and development *and* prioritize time, money, and energy for reaching out to the poor and excluded?

- **A Migrant Worker Mess** – As a community developer, Mary Ann quicky began to realize that she was wrestling with the tension of *either* supporting migrant workers *or* prioritizing farmers. Was it possible for her to offer advocacy to the farm workers *and* maintain solid relations with the neighbouring farmers?

Traditional problem solving would say no to all the above questions and choose one option over the other. Sadly, taking this Either/Or approach results in everybody losing out in the long term.

The reason I offer these examples is because I watched these people lead with AND, and as a result, they made the world a better place through their courageous leadership.

- By embracing *both* change *and* stability, Tim evolved the company into one that was awarded the second-best place to work in Canada and is focusing on meaningful work. As I'm writing this book, his organization is making a massive difference in the fight against COVID-19 *while at the same time* expanding internationally, growing rapidly, and shattering all sales and profit goals and expectations.

- By embracing *both* economic responsibility *and* social responsibility, Walter saw the city's downtown completely revitalized. St. Catharines enjoyed a boom in housing, tourism, and commercial investment *while at the same time* solidified a Compassionate City program that has been replicated in cities across the country.

- By caring for *both* migrant workers *and* farmers, Mary Ann found a way to become a trailblazer for migrant worker support outreach. Paving the road for hundreds of volunteers who would follow her lead, she met real needs for workers *while at the same time* became well-known, loved, and trusted by every farmer in the region.

I have had the privilege to work beside and learn from all three of these incredible leaders—individuals who chose to take the road less travelled yet didn't hit a dead end. These are leaders who had the wisdom to recognize that the challenges they faced were not problems to solve but tensions to manage instead.

They also had the courage to embrace Both/And thinking, and it resulted in their success.

Tensions 101

My first book, *The Power of Healthy Tension*,[2] focuses solely on what tensions are and how to manage them well. Beyond this, there is a long list of other great resources that can help you understand the phenomenon of tensions. The best, in my opinion, is from my friend and mentor, Dr. Barry Johnson, whose book, *Polarity Management*,[3] shaped my thinking and guides the content of this book.

Because you can access all of these other tension resources, I am not going to do a deep dive into the explanation of tensions in this book. I will only share with you this basic overview of what you need to know about tensions to fully engage and benefit from the upcoming chapters:

1. **Tensions are unsolvable.** Although the problem solver in you is going to want to find the right answer and make the tension disappear, don't be fooled! Successful leaders know that there are no 5 Habits, 7 Steps, or silver-bullet ideas that will solve the dilemma. It will be something you have to deal with as long as you are leading. The question is not, "Have I solved this?" Instead, it is, "Is this healthy or unhealthy?" Think of the metaphor of breathing, which requires the ongoing back and forth between inhaling and exhaling. This will never be "solved" until the day you die, yet the tension between inhaling and exhaling is a healthy one.

2. **Choosing one side won't work for long.** Again, although the problem solver in you yearns to choose a side and move on, this will backfire—every time. It's because the two sides of a tension are interdependent, meaning one side requires the other in order to be healthy. Successful leaders know that focusing on one side of a tension to the neglect of the other side will always undermine their vision and values. For example, overdone change to the neglect of stability will result in chaos and confusion. Overdone stability to the neglect of change will result in becoming stagnated and outdated.

3. **There's wisdom in resistance.** The problem solver in you will dislike resistance by default. It assumes that if people resist your thoughts, ideas, or values, they simply don't understand—or worse—they're against you. Successful leaders know, however, that when you're holding things in tension, someone who sees the situation from a different point of view has a perspective you need. Knowing that our blind spots can lead to vulnerable or even dangerous decision-making, the best way to move from seeing things from our limited point of view to understanding the whole truth is through the challenge, resistance, and push-back of others.

4. **It's not about compromise.** A problem-solving approach is all about winning, losing, or if necessary, compromising. However, compromising assumes you have to give up something on both

sides and meet somewhere in the middle, resulting in a lesser, watered-down version of each side's values. Successful leaders don't settle for compromise but instead find a way to gain all the positive results of both sides over time. It is worth noting that, although healthy tension is not about compromise, it does require a spirit of cooperation. We'll explore this concept deeper in future chapters.

5. **There's power in the word "and."** Problem solvers love to use the word "but" (and if you're a polite Canadian like me, "however" is the same thing). This means that when someone sees things from an opposite perspective that pushes back against our ideas, "but" is likely the first word out of our mouth. Unfortunately, the word "but" is one of the most polarizing words in the English language; it can push people away and make them feel like you are against them. Successful leaders choose to use the word "and" instead. "And" forces you to slow down your thinking, helps others realize you're not against them, and builds a bridge in your conversation instead of a wall.

Successful Leadership

Throughout the last decade, I've conducted some fascinating research. I've asked thousands of people in countries all over the world the same question: "When I say the word 'tension,' what is the first thing that comes to mind?" What I've consistently found, regardless of country, age, race, or gender, is that approximately

95% of the time, people go to a negative place. The words they immediately think of are words like conflict, stress, disagreement, headache, and pain. And because most people assume that tension is a bad thing, they do one of two things when they experience it: avoid it or ignore it.

Just like the muscles in our body are only able to become strong through tension and healthy stress, the best way to build resilience and deliver results is to learn how to hold things in tension.

Successful leaders, however, do the opposite; instead of avoiding or ignoring tension, they embrace it. They realize that tension is unavoidable in leadership and that it's a gift. Just like the muscles in our body are only able to become strong through tension and healthy stress, the best way to build resilience and deliver results is to learn how to hold things in tension. It's a successful leader's competitive edge.

Moving Forward

You now have the foundation you need to move forward into the core content of this book. As I previously mentioned, if you want to spend time learning more about the phenomenon of tensions, I strongly encourage you to check out the suggested resources at the end of this chapter. For the rest of this book, however, we are going to move from awareness to application.

Research would suggest that as a leader, there is a long list of tensions you are managing every single day, all of which require you to lead with AND. In the following chapters, though, we will only be focusing on six. It's not that the others don't matter, but these six are what I have found to be make-it-or-break-it ones for your leadership effectiveness. I've seen them as foundational to the success of Nobel Peace Prize winners and start-up entrepreneurs alike in my work as a consultant.

I've also found this to be true in my life as I attempt to lead. When I have really tried to move things forward and make the world a better place, success or failure has come down to how well I've been able to hold these things in tension. When life has been challenging, my level of resilience has been directly tied to how well I've been able to manage these tensions in the midst of the storm.

I am confident that these six leadership tensions will be relevant to you and become foundations to your success as a leader. Each of the following chapters will be devoted to one of the tensions:

- Being Optimistic AND Realistic
- Embracing Change AND Preserving Stability
- Being Profit Focused AND Purpose Driven
- Having Expectations AND Extending Grace
- Caring for Others AND Caring for Yourself
- Building Confidence AND Remaining Humble

You are about to 1. understand, 2. assess, and 3. leverage each of the six tensions so you can break through to a new level of resilience and results.

Let's do this!

- Book – *And: Making a Difference by Leveraging Polarity, Paradox or Dilemma* by Barry Johnson

- Book – *The Power of Healthy Tension* by Tim Arnold

- Online Course – The Power of Healthy Tension, www.leadersforleaders.ca/onlinecourse

To support you in growing your ability to tap into the power of healthy tension, take advantage of 50% off the normal price of the online course. Simply visit **www.leadersforleaders.ca/onlinecourse** and use the code HealthyTension to take advantage of this offer.

CHAPTER 3

THE FOUNDATIONS OF RESILIENCE

Being Optimistic AND Realistic

OPTIMISTIC – *Remaining hopeful and
resilient despite setbacks and challenges*

REALISTIC – *Facing the facts and remaining
objective, sensible, and practical*

The Blind Side, Part 1

It only took one volunteer shift at the local homeless shelter to unexpectedly realize I had stumbled into something quite significant. Although I had absolutely no lived experience with homelessness and had spent most of my life in a bubble of privilege and prosperity, the shelter surprisingly became a comfortable place for me, and the residents staying in the shelter quickly became unlikely friends.

To my surprise, I was so drawn to the shelter and working in the area of homelessness, I decided to move from being a volunteer to working in this field for a living. Within a very short time of my first volunteer shift, I sold the leadership development company and took on the role of Shelter Director.

The first few months in the shelter were a roller coaster ride of change, excitement, and vision. I was fortunate enough to work with an amazing team of dedicated professionals. Some came from a social service background, some had lived experience with homelessness, and some—like me—had little-to-no relevant training whatsoever.

We all, however, were passionate and committed to a shared vision. We were confident that very soon through our programs and services, our city would never be the same. We believed that our shelter was going to play a lead role in ending homelessness.

Sadly, what became clear by the end of the first year was that the Disney ending we all envisioned was proving to be somewhat naïve. Not that we didn't have amazing programs and services— we did! And we were seeing some incredible evidence of lives transformed through them. People were getting jobs, sustaining housing, overcoming addictions, and reuniting with family.

But that was only part of the story. We also found that what we offered didn't work for everyone, and in fact, some of the street-involved people we were reaching out to had no interest in our programs. We were also starting to grasp the true realities of mental illness, trauma, and the long-term impact of addictions. This meant that some of the people who walked through our doors would never have the ability to fit in with "normal" society, get a job, or sustain housing on their own.

Was our vision just wishful thinking? Was it time to face the facts and pare down our hopes and expectations? Was the best option simply to become yet another basic social service, to settle for just being OK? The answer wasn't fully yes or fully no.

STEP 1: UNDERSTAND

Most people think you are *either* optimistic *or* realistic by nature. You're naturally wired to see the glass as *either* half full *or* half empty. Successful leaders, however, believe this is simply untrue.

Right now, the world needs resilient leaders more than ever. We need visionary leaders who inspire those around them to have faith that our families, communities, and businesses will overcome in the end, regardless of how tough things get. We also need courageous leaders who can help their teams, friends, and families confront the brutal facts of the current reality, no matter how hard they are to face.

The Stockdale Principle

A great example of optimism and realism in action is Admiral Jim Stockdale who is featured in Jim Collins' ground-breaking book, *Good to Great.*[1] Stockdale spent eight years in a prisoner-of-war camp during the Vietnam War, enduring relentless psychological abuse and physical torture. He ultimately survived and went on to become the first three-star officer in the history of the Navy.

When Jim Collins interviewed Stockdale, he asked him how he was able to survive such tough circumstances when so many of his fellow soldiers did not. Stockdale said that it came down to two things:

> *"Successful leaders realize that optimism and realism only work well when working together; and this is not something that happens by chance, it's something that happens by choice."*

1. **Optimism** – "I never lost faith in the end of the story," he said. "I never doubted that I would get out, but also that I would prevail in the end and turn the experience into the defining event of my life, which in retrospect, I would not trade."

2. **Realism** – "There were some people who said, 'We're going to be out by Christmas.' And Christmas would come, and Christmas would go. Then they'd say, 'We're going to be out by Easter.' And Easter would come, and Easter would go. And then Thanksgiving, and then it would be Christmas again. And they died of a broken heart. You must never confuse faith that you will prevail in the end—which you can never afford to lose—with the discipline to confront the most brutal facts of your current reality, whatever they might be."

Like Stockdale, successful leaders realize that optimism and realism only work well when working together; and this is not something that happens by chance, it's something that happens by choice.

Optimism + Realism = Emotional Intelligence

For centuries, leadership development has focused on two things: your smarts and your skills. Conventional wisdom assumed that, to be a great leader, you needed a relatively high IQ, and you had to be well versed in a long list of skills—the kinds most MBA programs teach.

However, around 30 years ago, researchers were puzzled by the fact that some leaders were at the top of their class in terms of IQ and had more skills than they knew what to do with, yet they still struggled to lead effectively. They made unwise decisions that derailed their careers, they blew up every team they were a part of, and they couldn't maintain quality relationships. How could this be? If they had all the smarts and skills they needed to lead, what was missing?

This led to decades of research, all pointing to the fact that the missing ingredient to leadership effectiveness was emotional intelligence—or EQ—the social and emotional skills required to thrive. In his book, *Emotional Intelligence*,[2] author Daniel Goleman said,

> "The most effective leaders are all alike in one crucial way: they all have a high degree of what has come to be known as emotional intelligence. Without it, a person can have the best training in the world, an incisive, analytical mind, and an endless supply of smart ideas, but he still won't make a great leader."

He went on to say in one of Harvard Business Review's most enduring articles, "What Makes a Leader,"[3] "IQ gets you through the door, EQ dictates success."

We now have close to 30 years of research to back up this claim. From Harvard to Yale to the Center for Creative Leadership, study after study shows that people with high emotional intelligence are more effective leaders, outperform and earn more than their colleagues, have higher job satisfaction, and live with higher confidence, resilience, and happiness.

And what does it take to have a healthy level of EQ? There are quite a few ingredients to it; however, two key ones are optimism and reality-testing. Israeli psychologist Reuven Bar-On, the person who created the Bar-On EQ-i™,[4] which has become the gold standard in measuring emotional intelligence, defined and explained things this way:

Optimism – Positive attitude and outlook on life

- You approach the world with a "glass half full" attitude.
- You believe in yourself and others, and rarely give up prematurely.
- You inspire those you work with to overcome challenges.

Reality-testing – Objective; see things as they really are

- You are very unlikely to misinterpret critical information or allow emotions to color reality.
- You are keenly aware of your own strengths and weaknesses.
- You are attuned to your immediate environment and attentive to the task at hand.

Successful leaders know that book smarts and trained skills are not enough to be truly effective—it takes a healthy level of emotional intelligence as well. The great news about your EQ, as opposed to your IQ, is that it can be developed. This means that if you feel your optimism or realism needs to improve, it's 100% possible for you to develop these areas of EQ in your life.

Healthy Tension?

By now, it should be clear that finding a healthy tension between *both* optimism *and* realism is critical to leadership resilience and results. As the graphic below illustrates, there are positive results that can only come from embracing *both* optimism *and* realism, and there are negative results that are inevitable if you overdo one side to the neglect of the other.

TENSION

Being Optimistic and Being Realistic

 POSITIVE RESULTS OF BEING OPTIMISTIC

- Keeps morale high and fosters a "can-do" spirit
- Builds resilience to get through tough times
- Prepares team to take advantage of future opportunities

POSITIVE RESULTS OF BEING REALISTIC

- Has a "clear-eyed" view of the challenges being faced
- Makes sound (sometimes hard) decisions based on data
- Forces team to be innovative and adaptive

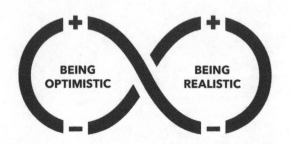

BEING OPTIMISTIC

BEING REALISTIC

NEGATIVE RESULTS WHEN OVERDONE —

- Avoids addressing the "cold hard facts"
- Team members lack trust in leader's competence
- Naïve approach results in vulnerability (or worse)

NEGATIVE RESULTS WHEN OVERDONE

- Creates a "doom and gloom" culture
- Missed opportunities because of rigid reliance on what is "safe and sound"
- Undermines effectiveness by getting lost in the details

Based on the Polarity Map® and Principles of Barry Johnson and Polarity Partnerships LLC

STEP 2: ASSESS

Reflect on your thoughts and actions this past season. Have you maintained a firm grasp on hope and lived in a place of high optimism? Have you been able to confront the brutal facts in front of you and embrace a high level of reality? Take a look at the following graphic and assess which of the four quadrants you are currently living in.

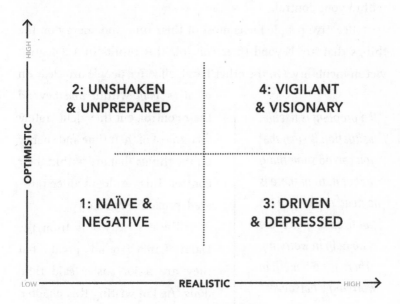

STEP 3: LEVERAGE

Regardless of what quadrant you currently find yourself in, the goal is to spend more and more time in quadrant four. The good news is that there are practical things you can do to gain the positive results of *both* optimism *and* realism as you become more vigilant and visionary.

Focus and Control

One of the best ways to hold optimism and realism in tension is to dust off a model so old it's almost new. In Stephen Covey's 1989 bestseller, *The 7 Habits of Highly Effective People*,[5] he introduces a model called Circles of Concern. The big idea is that effective leaders are mindful of what is within and beyond their control. Covey shows that for every challenge in life, you can quickly identify things that are beyond your control and things that are within your control.

Reactive people focus most of their time and energy on the things that are beyond their control. This results in a defeatist, victim mentality. On the other hand, effective people are clear on what is *both* within *and* beyond their control, but they deliberately focus most of their time and energy on the things that are within their control. This results in an empowered, proactive mentality.

> "If a problem is fixable, if a situation is such that you can do something about it, then there is no need to worry. If it's not fixable, then there is no help in worrying. There is no benefit in worrying whatsoever."
>
> DALAI LAMA

These wise words from the Dalai Lama sound great, but they are a lot easier said than done. As I'm writing this chapter, we're about 10 months into the COVID-19 pandemic, and Canada is experiencing the second wave, which is much worse than the first. We are in our second lockdown, so my kids are doing school at home, and my wife and I are both working from home. It's certainly a challenging time!

Here are a few examples of how Covey's Circles of Concern model relates to my current situation:

BEYOND MY CONTROL	WITHIN MY CONTROL
• Others' behaviour and actions (or lack of responsible actions) to help minimize the spread of COVID, save lives, and reopen the economy • Business closures and the declining stock market, and how this impacts my job and my investments • My inability to travel due to closed borders (knowing that a significant percentage of my work requires me to fly to corporate events)	• How I use the unexpected time I have due to work cancellations and postponements to work on projects I never seem to get to (such as finishing this book) • Making decisions around staffing, rent, travel, and subscriptions that will allow us to be leaner and run the business more efficiently • Pivoting and adapting our programs and services so they speak to real-time problems our clients are facing and solve these problems virtually

It is impossible to spend 100% of our time focused only on what we can control. In stressful and uncertain times, our minds can easily and quickly drift into a place of worry and anxiety around what-ifs and now-whats. That's OK! It's not helpful to beat yourself up. What is helpful is to recognize when this is happening and to learn how to quickly bring yourself back to a healthy, proactive place.

Successful leaders know that it is important to understand *both* what is within *and* what is beyond their control. There are things beyond your control that still have the ability to impact you, and you need to be prepared to deal with their impact. This grounds you in reality.

That said, there's wisdom in the words of John Maxwell, who said, "What we focus on expands." Once you've acknowledged and prepared for the impact of the things you can't control, you must learn to focus your time and energy on the things you can control. True optimism comes from refusing to be the victim but instead choosing to be the hero of your story—relentlessly focusing on the things you can control—so that despite significant challenges and obstacles, you win in the end.

> *"Grant me the serenity to accept the things I cannot change, courage to change the things I can, and wisdom to know the difference."*
>
> NIEBUHR

For almost 100 years, people in the world of addictions and recovery have recited a prayer to provide them with focus and encouragement. I think today, this is a prayer that all of us need to be reciting, sharing with others, and taking to heart: "Grant me the serenity to accept the things I cannot change, courage to change the things I can, and wisdom to know the difference."

AND LEADERSHIP IN ACTION
Allison Alley

Allison Alley is the president and chief executive officer of Compassion Canada. Compassion is one of the world's leading child development organizations with programs and services in over 25 countries aimed at ending poverty in the lives of children and their families. Through Compassion, over two million children are discovering lives full of promise and purpose as they receive support in all the different aspects of their lives: minds, bodies, and relationships.

To be successful, Allison needs to uphold the values of *both* optimism *and* realism every day in her role as a leader and within teams across the organization. I had a chance to ask Allison some questions on the ways she taps into healthy tension between optimism and realism. Her answers are not only incredibly insightful, but contain ideas you can put into practice yourself.

Action Steps[6]

What are things that you do to gain the positive results of optimism?

- **Systematize the present.** There are great things happening in the organization every single day, even in the hardest of times. Make sure people are aware of these signs of progress. We build programs and systems across the organization to capture and share these everyday wins. This includes a Thankful Thursday activity each team conducts weekly and a Good News Channel that is updated with stories from staff and the people we serve every single day.

- **Set short-term goals.** Our vision of ending poverty isn't going to happen any time soon, which means that team members need quick wins to stay optimistic and hopeful. Leaders must set "lead goals" for their team on things they have direct control over. Seeing these short-term goals achieved and celebrating the success together allows team members to realize they are having real impact, and things are moving in a good direction.

- **Reiterate the vision.** Remind people ad nauseum about the big picture and where we're headed as an organization. People need to be constantly clear on—and inspired by—our vision. This reinforces why our hard work and struggles right now are important and will be worth it in the end.

What are things you do to gain the positive results of realism?

- **Name the challenge.** As a leader, you must call things out and create a shared language and common understanding around the challenges you face as an organization. Through regular town halls, I spend a considerable amount of time talking about the real-time challenges we're facing and how these challenges may impact us.

- **Democratize knowledge.** As leaders, we make almost all company data and strategy accessible to employees across the organization, regardless of their role or department. This puts everyone on a level playing field and allows team members to feel they are always "in the know." This also means that individual and team workplans are shared knowledge to ensure everyone is clear on where we're going collectively *and* individually.

- **Stay tuned in.** Every week, I carve out 90 minutes to host Coffee with Allison where I sit down with four random staff members from across the organization. With the value of radical candour[7] (caring

personally and challenging directly), I share with
them where we are as an organization and what
I believe is coming around the corner. I also ask
team members to share with me one thing that they
think I don't know but should know, and one thing
we're not talking about as an organization that they
believe we should be.

Red Flags[8]

What are early warning signs that you're overfocusing on optimism to the neglect of realism?

- **Overdone Agreement** – When I notice that our
  team meetings are becoming overly nice and seem to
  be filled with too much consensus, I get concerned.
  Meetings exist for sharing diverse opinions, fostering
  healthy debate, and making challenging decisions.
  When I see these things starting to disappear from
  our meetings, we talk about why this is happening
  and what we need to do to fix the situation.

- **Misaligned Perception** – Something I pay a lot
  of attention to is anytime I hear the phrase, "I just
  don't think you understand," from staff members.
  Even if I disagree with them and feel I understand
  the situation or challenge incredibly well, their
  perception of my understanding is their reality (and
  is probably the reality of other staff as well). I make
  sure I listen to them and learn what they feel I need
  to know, and what they believe we should be doing
  about the situation. These conversations often result

in a new or better way we can communicate around current challenges we are facing.

What are early warning signs that you're overfocusing on realism to the neglect of optimism?

- **Loss of Story** – We put a lot of energy into knowing the data and making sure our meetings and communications are data informed. However, I pay close attention anytime I hear feedback from staff or donors that our meetings or communications feel boring or lack energy and inspiration. This often points to data overpowering our story and vision.

- **Running on Empty** – We have super-high expectations on each team member and realize that their jobs require them to navigate heavy issues that include poverty and injustice. Despite this, our workplace culture is normally incredibly positive and engagement is high. So, I pay close attention anytime I feel a sense of pessimism and fatigue in team members or during meetings. This is often a red flag that we need to find ways to boost our optimism and positivity.

The Blind Side, Part 2

As I mentioned at the beginning of this chapter, it didn't take long for our team at the homeless shelter to realize that our mission and vision were somewhat naïve. We found we had to let go of our expectation for a perfect ending in everyone's life; however, this didn't mean giving up our core value of optimism. It simply meant that we had to learn to hold this value in tension with realism.

To quote the wise words of my friend and mentor, Dion Oxford, "to live a happy life, everyone needs (and deserves) a friend, a job, and a home." Optimistically, we believed that our programs and services could help ensure all our street-involved friends who walked through the doors of the shelter could achieve these things in their lives. However, having a solid grasp on reality meant we knew that what a friend, a job, and a home looked like to most people would probably be *very* different than what it would like for the folks we served.

Due to mental health challenges and the impact of addictions and trauma, many of our residents may never have the ability to sustain a long list of Facebook friends, yet, through our recreational programs, they could authentically connect with a few caring volunteers who would prove to be there for them unconditionally. They may never have the resources or independence to buy a home or secure an apartment on their own, but through the right programs and planning, they could sustain supportive housing and call a place their own. They may not have the social skills or the mental health to sustain "normal" employment, but they could contribute meaningfully in an ongoing way to one of our social enterprises.

What was interesting was that when I started my leadership role in the shelter, I was determined to create a culture of excellence. Over time, however, I found that through being *both* optimistic *and* realistic, excellence wasn't the value that we needed to strive for. Instead, we were living out a superior culture that would be much better defined by one word: beauty. We were embracing all the values of optimism, hope, and vision while at the same time courageously facing the realities of street involvement, brokenness, and pain. And all that combined to produce something truly beautiful.

ADDITIONAL RESOURCES

- Book – *The 7 Habits of Highly Effective People* by Stephen Covey (Habit #1)

- Book – *Emotional Intelligence* by Daniel Goleman

- Assessment – BarOn EQ-i, https://www.reuvenbaron.org

CHAPTER 4

OUTSMARTING CHANGE

Embracing Change AND Preserving Stability

CHANGE – *To undergo transformation or transition.*
To take a different position, course, or direction.

STABILITY – *The strength to stand or endure. Firmly*
established, steady in purpose, and firm in resolution.

The Problem with Pivoting, Part 1

The year 2020 started out so well! My business had finally settled into a great place of impact and profitability. Our leadership development programs were well designed and directly helping to solve the problems our clients were facing. The business model was strategic in not having all our eggs in one basket: team workshops accounted for about a third of the business, keynote speaking accounted for another third, and the final third was custom projects for clients. What made all of this even more fantastic is that we were loving the work we were delivering and the small team that we got to do it with. After years of

It was becoming clear to me that this crisis was different than anything I had experienced before, and I was about to fly home to a new reality.

hard work, things were finally at a stable and successful place.

And then came COVID-19.

It didn't seem like a big deal for the first few months. I'd been running businesses long enough to know that these kinds of disruptions happen, and over time, everything works out. I thought of the numerous stock market busts I'd lived through, and remembered the initial impact of 9/11. Like those difficult seasons, I knew that this too shall pass.

But my level of concern changed the evening of Wednesday, March 11. I was having dinner at a hotel restaurant in Calgary, Alberta, preparing to deliver a workshop the next morning, when things started to go off the rails. Tom Hanks and his wife, Rita Wilson, both tested positive for COVID-19. A few hours later, the NBA announced they were suspending all games indefinitely. The next morning, it was announced that schools would be closed in the province where I lived. That evening, as I walked down one of the main corridors in the Calgary International Airport, there was not a person in sight. It was becoming clear to me that this crisis was different than anything I had experienced before, and I was about to fly home to a new reality.

Within one week, 75% of our leadership development workshops, keynotes, and consulting projects were cancelled or postponed indefinitely. Every proposal I was working on was dead, and the phone stopped ringing. What made this even more terrifying was only about 20% of our work was delivered virtually. The other 80% involved flying to the workshop location, meeting in large conference centres, and bringing lots of people together—close together. None of these things were possible anymore, and it didn't look like they would be possible anytime soon.

Within no time, the word that I started to hear numerous times every day was "pivot." It didn't matter if you were scrolling through LinkedIn, having a Zoom meeting with colleagues, or listening to a business podcast, you'd hear it again and again: How are you pivoting? What's your pivot strategy? Pivot, PIVOT, PIVOT!*

For our team, however, the thought of pivoting had us somewhat paralyzed. The business was in a great place and had been thriving at every level. We were really good at what we did, and our clients trusted us because of it. We had narrowed down what we offered to a short list of leadership content we 100% believed in, practised personally, and knew had impact. Delivering a keynote on the main stage or a workshop in the meeting room was our sweet spot.

In our minds, online delivery would potentially make us vulnerable to mediocrity. Moving our programs online meant having to fully redesign them. Should we just wait it out and hope that things would get back to normal in the months ahead? Or should we embrace a pivot strategy of our own and shift to virtual workshops and keynotes?

STEP 1: UNDERSTAND

Most people think you must choose between leading like Steve Jobs and develop an Apple culture that is known for innovation, speed, and change, or you must lead like Sam Walton and develop

---

* For those of you who now need to see the "pivot" episode of *Friends*, it's the 16th episode of Season 5.

a Walmart culture that is known for consistency, solidity, and stability. Successful leaders, however, prove that this Either/Or approach is a setup and choose a much better path.

Embracing Change

I don't think I fully grasped how true "change is the law of life" really was until I became a father. My life certainly changed on almost every level—my schedule, my priorities, my finances, and my self-preoccupation. What was even more powerful, though,

> *"Change is the law of life. And those who look only to the past or present are certain to miss the future."*
>
> JOHN F. KENNEDY

was watching the nonstop changes in my kids. This was true at a physical level: bald heads soon had sprigs of hair, no teeth became baby teeth and then adult teeth (and of course braces), small and fragile bodies quickly became tall and strong. It was also true of their abilities: from sitting to crawling to walking to running, from picking up their spoon to throwing a ball to writing their names to learning how to drive. At times, it felt as though if I had to be away more than a few days on business, I was likely to miss something.

And the fact that change happens is not just true at home, it's true of everything around us. Seasons continue to come and go, the sun and moon never stay in one place, and the daily headline is always updating us on something new. Change truly is the law of life.

Accordingly, change should be the law of your organization as well. If you pause to look around and notice that things don't seem to be changing, innovating, or evolving, you should be very, *very* concerned. A lack of change signals stagnation and death.

Healthy organizations are mission and vision driven. As a leader, you are committed to living out your mission of helping your customers solve their problems. You're guided by the vision of a better future due to the impact of your work. Being mission and vision driven means you must *always* be moving forward, taking new steps, testing new paths, and trying out new ways to progress. If your organization or your team is not constantly changing and innovating, you are not gaining any ground on achieving your vision, and you are (or soon will be) getting left behind by someone else who is.

Change is also energy. During COVID-19, as a grade one educator, my wife, Becky, had to leave her classroom and teach online during a few months of lockdown. This meant learning and relying on new virtual technologies, modifying lesson plans, and adopting new teaching techniques. The learning curve was steep, and it was an incredibly challenging, stressful season.

But something really cool happened: teachers started collaborating! They shared best practices, made their lesson plans public domain, and started doing after-school Zoom check-ins each day to encourage and support one another.

About a month into the lockdown, Becky told me that it was the most change she'd ever experienced in her career, *and* it was also the healthiest team culture she'd ever experienced. She said the positive energy, the level of teamwork, and the commitment to making things work was unlike anything she had experienced in her 15 years of teaching. As much as she looked forward to returning to the classroom, she hoped that somehow their staff could hold on to the positive energy that the change had allowed them to tap into.

There is an energy generated in times of change and innovation that is life giving. It heightens engagement, creates excitement, and makes the day pass quickly. A lack of change kills this energy. Boredom sets in and positivity is replaced with complacency and a feeling of just getting by.

Preserving Stability

I remember when I was working for an extended period of time out of the country, I would occasionally receive a care package in the mail. All it took was something as simple as a Canadian chocolate bar that I hadn't seen or tasted for a few months, or some clippings from our small local newspaper, and I would feel a sense of comfort and connection. The stable and safe feeling of home—a feeling we all need in our lives—brought me much peace.

As a trainer, I sometimes get the opportunity to deliver the same leadership development program over and over again. This happens when I roll out a workshop to an entire department or throughout the organization. By the fourth or fifth delivery of the program, I feel so confident and skilled. I know what questions to expect and how to answer them before they are asked. I know what parts of the program are most relevant and when to spend extra time in those areas. I know what lines will get a laugh and am sure to never leave those lines out. I am an expert in my craft, and as a result, the client is the ultimate winner.

"When stability becomes a habit, maturity and clarity follow."

B.K.S. IYENGAR

This level of mastery only comes through repetition and stability. If I'm always designing and delivering new programs, mastery is impossible to achieve. Similarly, your team and organization cannot be truly great at what they do in an industry-leading way without a healthy level of consistency and stability.

As a consultant, I get to come alongside hundreds of organizations and peek behind the curtain to see their true corporate culture. As you'd expect, I've seen good, bad, and downright ugly. However, without fail, the cultures that stand out as the healthiest and most productive always have two things in common:

1. Their mission and vision are crystal clear and understood by all. Despite the change and innovation that teams may be pursuing to achieve this mission and vision, the mission and vision themselves—or the "why" of the company—are unwavering. This results in every employee having the stability they need to experience the clarity, safety, and security you'd see in a healthy home.

2. The companies also don't get distracted by every new and shiny object (i.e., the new opportunity of the day, client fads, industry trends, etc.). Instead, they are laser focused on doing a few things incredibly well. This gives staff the ability to become masters and leaders in their fields.

A Perfect Blend

Although all families have some level of dysfunction, some are a lot healthier than others. Think of the healthiest family you were close to growing up. (I hope it was your family, but it doesn't have to be.) I bet there was a lot of stability in that family. I bet that things like unconditional love and support were never questioned, and the children always felt a sense of safety and security as a result. I bet there was some consistency in how the family worked and what was expected of one another, and there were some basic house rules that everyone knew and understood.

I also bet this family truly lived life and embraced change on many levels. I expect that the parents were not overprotective and didn't hold their kids back from growing up and experiencing the world, but let them figure many things out on their own, even the hard way if necessary. I bet there was a sense of fun and adventure in the household that came from not playing things too safe.

What's true at home is every bit as true in our organizations: To be healthy and stand out from the crowd, we must learn to find a great combination of both change and stability.

Healthy Tension?

By now, I hope it's clear that navigating the tension between *both* change *and* stability is critical to leadership resilience and results. As the graphic below illustrates, there are positive results that can only come from embracing each side, and there are negative results that are inevitable if you overdo one side to the neglect of the other.

TENSION

Embracing Change and Preserving Stability

＋ POSITIVE RESULTS OF **CHANGE**

- Stay relevant and responsive to new realities
- Leverage emerging opportunities and new ways of working
- Adapt our goals to ensure we don't get left behind

POSITIVE RESULTS OF **STABILITY** ＋

- Maintain product and service quality
- Create a sense of consistency and confidence
- Ensure core values and best practices don't get lost

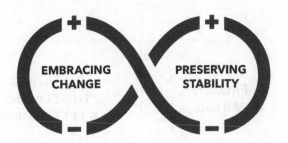

EMBRACING CHANGE

PRESERVING STABILITY

－ NEGATIVE RESULTS WHEN **OVERDONE**

- Lose sight of what we are known for and best practices
- Live in a state of chaos and confusion
- Make poor decisions that have long-term impacts

NEGATIVE RESULTS WHEN **OVERDONE** －

- Unable to stay relevant and helpful when things change
- Miss out on opportunities outside of existing plans
- Inability to achieve goals leads to business failure

STEP 2: ASSESS

Reflect on your thoughts and actions this past season. Have you put effort into staying relevant and embracing change and innovation? Have you been deliberate in holding on to what matters and maintaining a culture of consistency and stability? Take a look at the following graphic and assess which of the four quadrants you are currently living in.

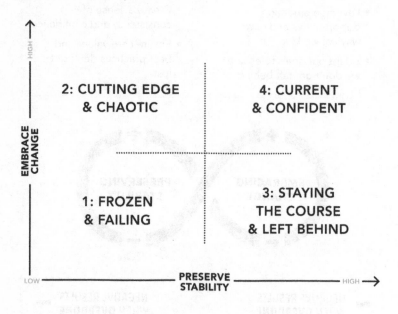

STEP 3: LEVERAGE

Regardless of what quadrant you currently find yourself in, the goal is to spend more and more time in quadrant four. Thankfully, there are practical things you can do to gain the positive results of *both* change *and* stability as you become more current and confident.

The Change Cycle

Since the 1930s, studies have suggested that only 30% to 40% of organizational change initiatives result in the successful outcomes expected, and a high percentage have unexpected negative results. Although there are many factors contributing to this, one key factor is that, although people may have been prepared for how the change would look, they weren't prepared for how the change would feel.

Some of the most helpful insights into how change feels come from psychiatrist Elisabeth Kübler-Ross. She is the author of the internationally best-selling book, *On Death and Dying*,[1] where she provided the ground-breaking theory of the stages of grief, also known as the Kübler-Ross model.

This is an adapted, four-stage version of her work:

THE CHANGE CYCLE

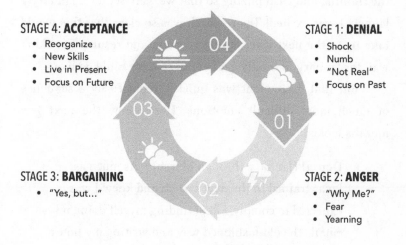

STAGE 4: **ACCEPTANCE**
- Reorganize
- New Skills
- Live in Present
- Focus on Future

STAGE 1: **DENIAL**
- Shock
- Numb
- "Not Real"
- Focus on Past

STAGE 3: **BARGAINING**
- "Yes, but..."

STAGE 2: **ANGER**
- "Why Me?"
- Fear
- Yearning

Thanks to Elisabeth Kubler Ross, On Death and Dying, *1969*

> *The very best way to outsmart change and ensure your team doesn't get stuck in the denial and anger phases is to hold change in tension with stability.*

Kübler-Ross would suggest that when people experience a change in their lives, these steps are predictable and unavoidable. It is simply an aspect of human nature. Although her work focused on the grieving process associated with losing a loved one, this cycle of response turned out to be true with most changes in our lives, including changes in the workplace.

I'll share with you a personal example of my journey through this cycle. Recently, after realizing that my do-it-yourself spreadsheet approach to customer relationship management (CRM) was not serving our team or our customers well, I decided to invest in a quality CRM solution. After some research, we decided to subscribe to Salesforce. My associate, Claudia, did all the training and customizing so that we were set for a January 1 launch. I was excited! The research was so clear that this would take us to the next level of effectiveness and results. I couldn't wait for January to finally get here so that we could go live.

But that excitement was quickly replaced by a sequence of much more difficult emotions. Here's how the next few months looked:

- **Denial** (January through March) – As much as I was trained in the new system and knew I was expected to comply, I kept finding myself doing my emails the old-fashioned way and writing my notes on the same notepad I had used for years.

- **Anger** (April) – After it became clear at the quarterly team meeting that I was lagging in my compliance, I committed to get with the program. But every day, I would complain (often in my head) about how much I missed the old way of doing things, how complicated this new system was, and how much money this subscription was costing us.

- **Bargaining** (May through June) – I was living in two worlds. For efficiency reasons (or so I thought), I would often go with my old pad-and-paper approach, and then at the end of the day, I'd convert things to the CRM system. I was starting to see the benefits Salesforce provided the more I pushed myself to use it, but I also felt most confident in my old way of doing things.

- **Acceptance** (July onwards) – It soon became clear that the new system was more effective and was resulting in more success. It was also becoming clear that it was actually an easier system than my old approach. I had finally committed to a new way of doing things.

What's interesting about my personal example of going through Kübler-Ross' stages is that it was a change I actually wanted. In fact, I wanted the change so badly that I was investing significant resources to make it happen. Imagine how much more profoundly I would've struggled if the change was one I didn't support or understand, or one that I feared!

The very best way to outsmart change and ensure your team doesn't get stuck in the denial and anger phases is to hold change in tension with stability. Strategizing how you will hold onto the value of stability as you embrace a change, and then communicating this strategy to team members, will help reduce their fears that the change will cost them the sense of safety and security they need.

Also, by acknowledging the potential downsides of over-done change before these downsides show up, team members will work with you (instead of against you) during the bargaining phase to ensure these downsides are avoided. All of this moves the organization into the phase of acceptance in a faster and healthier way.

AND LEADERSHIP IN ACTION
Tim Schurrer

As the chief operating officer at StoryBrand, Tim Schurrer has assembled a team of people who accomplish lofty goals and world-changing vision by breaking them down into practical, daily actions. As a result, StoryBrand has consulted with dozens of billion-dollar brands and thousands of small businesses, helping them dramatically increase their revenue through clarifying their message.

To be successful, Tim needs to uphold the values of *both* change *and* stability every day—and ensure that the teams across the organization are doing so as well.

Recently, I had a chance to ask Tim some questions about the ways in which he taps into the healthy tension between change and stability. His answers are not only incredibly insightful, but contain ideas you can put into practice as well.

Action Steps

What are things that you do to gain the positive results of change?

- **Reinforce the mission.** You need a clear statement repeated ad nauseum and memorized by every single staff member. When we pivot, we update our mission statement and make it incredibly clear by using this formula: *We will accomplish X by Y because of Z.* For example, *we will have 250,000 people on our online platform by December 31, 2024, because everybody deserves the help they need to grow their business.* Unless everyone has this message completely metabolized, they will not fully embrace the change with you.

- **Create a one-pager.** To ensure clarity and buy-in around the change, we give every staff member a one-page document using this format:

  - The company goals are at the top. (See the bullet point above for the mission formula.)

  - Under these goals is the heading "My Department's Top Priorities" with a short list of one to five priorities linked to the mission.

  - Under that is the heading "My Personal Priorities" with a short list of one to five items each team member is responsible for contributing to the team and the mission.

○ Finally, we include a "My Development Plan" section with a short list of one to three areas of development for each team member to ensure their success.

We bring these one-pagers into our daily stand-up meetings, which are structured around updates on each person's contribution. We ask, "What did each person get done since we last met? What is each person working on next? Is anything standing in her/his way or keeping her/him from doing the work?"[*]

What are things you do to gain the positive results of stability?

- **Minimize confusion.** People will jump to their own conclusions if you let them. When they learn about change happening in the organization and fear the risk associated with the change, a scarcity mindset can easily lead them to assume a) you're going to lose what matters as an organization (e.g., core values, reputation, etc.), and b) you're on a one-way path into the land of chaos and confusion.

Don't let this happen! You need constant communication on the "why" behind the change, and

---

[*] For a template of this one-pager, refer to *Business Made Simple* in the Additional Resources offered at the end of this chapter.

how this "why" is directly linked to the values and vision you've always been pursuing. You also must have constant communication on the "how" of the change so that staff understand how the path ahead will continue to be strategic, structured, and stable, despite the change.

- **Find beauty in structure.** As a relatively new parent, I've been amazed at how my kids thrive on routine and structure. I think that, in many ways, we never outgrow this need for rhythm and routine. In a season of change, I am deliberate in ensuring we have *more* one-on-one conversations, team meetings, and all-staff updates than normal, and that these are prioritized and scheduled so staff come to rely on them. They create an ongoing structure of safety and stability for staff, giving them the clarity they need to be confident.

Red Flags

What are early warning signs that you're overfocusing on change to the neglect of stability?

- **Mission Confusion** – People can't read your mind, and they won't remember what you said if they only hear it one or two times. I routinely go around the organization and ask random people to tell me what they believe to be the number-one goal of the organization right now and how we plan to achieve it. If they don't tell me the exact same thing we would say as leaders, I see that as a huge red flag that we're moving too fast. And this does not mean that the staff just "don't get it" or are "not on board." It means we have a communication and pace-setting problem. As a leader, it's *my* responsibility to ensure that the staff understand where we're going and why.

- **Rework** – When I hear a team (or team member) voicing frustration over a project they need to redo or backpedal on because it no longer fits with our current strategy, this normally points to the fact that people are working too fast and are not communicating between teams and departments about how their work needs to align to achieve our current mission.

What are early warning signs that you're overfocusing on stability to the neglect of change?

- **Life Is (Too) Good** – My mind goes to the words of author Andrew Grove[2] who wisely said, "Only the paranoid survive." The leaders of the company have to constantly feel like something is in their blind spot. If you are sitting in a place of total comfort and stability, I think the countdown clock has already started, and things are going to end for you quite quickly. As a leader, there is predatory conflict and competition on your heels all the time. You can sit down and rest, but you had better know that you ran a lot faster than them in the last leg of the race and be calculating how long you have until they catch up.

- **Spinning Your Wheels** – You start to confuse activity with results. You get content with the busyness of your routine (e.g., meetings, client work, etc.) but fail to realize that none of this is moving things forward. You need to have metrics in place that constantly let you know if you're making real progress as you set out to achieve your goals.

The Problem with Pivoting, Part 2

As I mentioned at the beginning of this chapter, COVID-19 forced us to make a huge decision as a company: Should we stay the course with the leadership content we were known for and had proven to deliver results, or should we pivot and shift to offering a new line of virtual workshops and keynotes?

The answer was...YES!

It became clear that the world wasn't going back to normal anytime quickly, and we realized that if we didn't move all of our programs and services to online delivery, we wouldn't survive. So, we decided to fully embrace change.

The best part of this story is that by embracing change and preserving stability, we ended up with our biggest year in both sales and profitability by far.

Within two weeks of COVID-19 being declared a pandemic, our company was reinvented. On our homepage, pictures of groups giving each other high fives were replaced with happy faces in a Zoom meeting, and our tagline now read, "Virtual Team Building & Leadership Development." Our normal half-day and full-day workshop format was replaced with a series of one-hour sessions so clients didn't have to stare at a screen too long.

However, we knew that we had to hold onto what we were known for and to ensure our quality for our clients was better than ever. So, to preserve the element of stability, we paired down the long list of in-person workshop options to a short list of virtual workshops that we knew would be relevant in this COVID-19 world. This focused approach allowed us to put in the research and design that was required to ensure every virtual workshop was amazing and exceeded our client's expectations.

The deliberate effort we put into *both* embracing change *and* preserving stability paid off. Within one month, we were commonly getting calls from new clients referred by existing clients who told them that we did virtual training better than anyone else. We unexpectedly became known as leaders in virtual team and leadership development.

Beyond that, our paired down programming turned out to be the highest quality work we've ever delivered (so far). The best part of this story is that by embracing change and preserving stability, we ended up with our biggest year in *both* sales *and* profitability by far. We chose to lead with AND and tapped into the power of healthy tension.

ADDITIONAL RESOURCES

- Book – *Business Made Simple: 60 Days to Master Leadership, Sales, Marketing, Execution, Management, Personal Productivity and More* by Donald Miller

CHAPTER 5

BIG DREAMS VERSUS THE BOTTOM LINE

Being Profit Focused AND Purpose Driven

PROFIT – *A financial gain, especially the difference between the amount earned and the amount spent in buying, operating, or producing something*

PURPOSE – *Why you do something or why something exists. An intended or desired result.*

When Money Matters, Part 1

After a 10-year run leading my first company, I knew it was time to make a change. Up until that time, I had been travelling all over the world building teams and developing leaders, and loving almost every minute of it. However, I realized that I was starting to feel a bit bored with my work. Knowing my team and my clients deserved a fully engaged leader, I started to explore what my next move should be.

Outside of work, I had been putting in a ton of hours as a volunteer at a local homeless shelter that was still in start-up mode. At the time, they were searching for a director to run the shelter, and in a very unexpected turn of events, I was given the opportunity of stepping into that role.

My only working experience to that point had been in the world of for-profit business and entrepreneurship. The charitable, not-for-profit world was completely foreign to me and came with a lot of unexpected challenges. The challenge that kept me up at night was the chasm between the abundance of vision our team had and the lack of funding available to live this vision out.

We operated from a budget that was made up government funding and community donations. Our government partners were clear that they would fund about 70% of what it would cost to feed and house the 40 people per night we served. The rest had to come from donations. This meant that our community fund-raising was aimed at making up the other 30%, allowing us to just get by financially.

Just get by?! That wasn't what I had signed up for. We wanted to be visionary! We wanted to launch innovative new programs and services that would help get people off the streets for good. We wanted to upgrade our facility so it was "hotel quality," show-ing our street-involved friends their true value and worth.

When I talked to team members about how to deal with this dilemma, there were a variety of opinions—none of which I felt good about. Some who had worked in the social service world for years would tell me to just get used to it because "getting by" is how things work. Others would suggest chasing grant money, but that meant mountains of paperwork and modifying our vision to meet the requirements of the grant. Still others suggested we look at corporate partnerships, but that often came with a lot of strings attached, which didn't feel appropriate for our community.

Was I missing something? Was there another option that would allow us to stay true to our purpose and live out our vision, but do this in a way that was financially sustainable?

STEP 1: UNDERSTAND

We are conditioned to believe that some people (and organizations) are all about making money—the 1%, the greedy, and the privileged—while others are all about making a difference—servant-leaders, humanitarians, and charities. What if the most powerful strategy for long-term impact is to pursue *both*? What if profit and purpose are the best formulas to change the world?

What Is Your Why?

In his ground-breaking book, *Start with Why,*[1] Simon Sinek explains how most leaders and organizations are clear on their "what"—the products and services they sell. They are also clear on their "how"—the things that make them special or set them apart from the crowd. Unfortunately, however, most leaders are unclear on their "why"—their purpose, cause, or belief, and their very reason for existence.

He goes on to clearly demonstrate how the leaders who've had the greatest influence in the world, people like Martin Luther King Jr., Steve Jobs, and the Wright Brothers, all started with "why." They knew that people wouldn't truly buy into their product, service, movement, or idea until they understood the "why" behind it. They were constantly communicating their "why." They

> *Most leaders are unclear on their 'why'– their purpose, cause, or belief, and their very reason for existence.*

inspired their teams, attracted customers, and grew their businesses based on their "why." Having clarity around their "why" and keeping it top of mind was the key to staying driven and inspired to make a difference.

Are you clear on your "why?" Can you confidently articulate what it is you do that is essential to your customers' or clients' surviving and thriving? Is this what gets you out of bed in the morning and pushes you through the inevitable hard times and setbacks every leader faces?

Essential Services

During the first few months of COVID-19, everyone seemed to be talking about what was and what wasn't deemed an essential service. People were wondering who would make the government essential services lists and be able to continue with business as usual despite lockdowns and restrictions. Did their service qualify? Would they still have a job during this time of crisis?

In Canada, an essential service is defined as "a service, the interruption of which would endanger the life, health, or personal safety of the whole or part of the population." Like my business, many of your organizations wouldn't qualify as essential based on that definition; however, don't let that trick you into thinking you're not in fact essential from a broader view.

Regardless of whatever government list you are (or aren't) a part of, there should be something essential about what you do, *both* for your clients *and* for your team. Without this purpose, why are you in business in the first place?

One of my all-time favorite books is *Essentialism: The Disciplined Pursuit of Less*,[2] by Greg McKeown. Greg defines an essentialist as someone who is disciplined around discerning what is absolutely essential then eliminating everything that is not. As a leader, this means that out of everything you do, you're incredibly clear on the core way you serve others—your true purpose.

Essentialists also examine the ways they are spending their time and energy that are not having as much impact. And they are quick to eradicate those things. Less is more! This philosophy looks to constantly find more ways to do the things that are making a difference and work hard to eliminate the things that are not, thereby becoming more purpose driven every day.

How can you apply this philosophy to yourself?

- Out of everything you do, which service you provide is most critical to your clients' surviving and thriving? How much are you focusing your time and energy on providing that service, regardless of their ability to pay for it?

- How much of your time is being wasted on things that are non-essential? How committed are you to ending those things, even if they bring in a lot of money?

These are the questions I think every leader needs to have clear answers to. As a leader who is purpose driven, how can you focus on what matters most to make a difference in the lives of those who need it most?

Paying the Bills

Living out your "why" and being purpose driven is a lot more enjoyable when you're not constantly worried about making rent.

In fact, beyond the peace of mind that comes with sustainability, when your purpose actually starts to become a profitable venture, you are able to impact the world in a much greater way.

It's been 14 years since I sold my first company. Every now and then, I run into one of my original employees and get the updates on all that is happening with the company these days. New hires on the team, new program lines being launched, and new client relationships being developed. The company is exponentially larger and more diverse than it was when I was in charge, which is always exciting to hear.

I find myself leaving these conversations feeling so fascinated by the power of a profitable business. I think of all the jobs that these businesses have created that enable people to do work they love, support their family, and buy homes. On a grander level, I think of how these jobs contribute to the local economy and help to bring in the taxes needed to make our communities and our country thrive. Paying attention to the bottom line and working hard to be profitable results in so many people winning out in the end.

Ensuring profitability also means you can reach so many more people with the essential service you provide. With the ability to make smart investments in infrastructure and equipment, you can achieve greater program or service quality. The ability to hire the right people allows you to expand your reach in terms of the sheer number of people you can serve, the demographics you can impact, and the geography you can cover. Profitability allows your purpose to expand its reach and impact.

Walking Our Talk

As I mentioned in the previous chapter, when COVID-19 hit us in March of 2020, our company went from being overwhelmed with work to having two months of absolutely no work whatsoever. It was the first crisis that I faced in the business since 9/11, and it had me wondering if we'd be able to survive.

Our team knew it was a time to practise what we preached to our clients and tap into the tension between being *both* profit focused *and* purpose driven. This meant, on one hand, we had to look at the bottom line and make changes to goals, targets, and plans that would ensure short-term survival and enable long-term success. On the other hand, we had to step back and ask ourselves, out of all our clients, who did we have a duty of care to help through this crisis, regardless of their ability to pay us? And how could we make it our mission to serve them with the essential service we provided in the months ahead?

Fast forward one full year and the business has never been stronger. The bottom-line focus on profitability resulted in us becoming a much more lean and efficient company. The commitment to living out our "why" and being purpose driven, regardless of payment, resulted in stronger and more committed client relationships than we've ever experienced. It also resulted in a huge upswing in unsolicited referrals and positive word of mouth.

Being profit focused and purpose driven is challenging. It takes ongoing, deliberate attention and action. However, it's the best path toward a life of making a living *and* making a difference.

Healthy Tension?

By now, it should be clear that finding healthy tension between *both* profit *and* purpose is critical to leadership resilience and results. As the graphic below illustrates, there are positive results that can only come from being profit focused and being purpose driven; and there are negative results that are inevitable if you overdo one side to the neglect of the other.

TENSION
Being Profit Focused and Purpose Driven

➕ POSITIVE RESULTS OF BEING **PROFIT FOCUSED**

- Business is sustainable and jobs are secure
- Goals and targets create a motivating culture
- Creates opportunity for growth and greater impact

POSITIVE RESULTS OF BEING **PURPOSE DRIVEN** ➕

- The business makes a real difference in the world
- A clear "why" creates focus and drives decision making
- Staff engagement and motivation are high

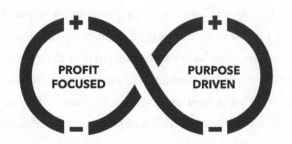

PROFIT FOCUSED

PURPOSE DRIVEN

➖ NEGATIVE RESULTS WHEN **OVERDONE**

- Impact in the world is limited by financial goals
- Lack of clarity around what business to focus on
- Low staff engagement because work lacks purpose

NEGATIVE RESULTS WHEN **OVERDONE** ➖

- Business is not sustainable and jobs are jeopardized
- Missed targets and cost overruns
- Financial irresponsibility creates staff insecurity

STEP 2: ASSESS

Reflect on your thoughts and actions this past season. Have you kept your eye on the bottom line and worked hard to become more profitable? Have you been deliberate in keeping things aligned to the "why" of your work and the purpose that drives you? Take a look at the following graphic and assess which of the four quadrants you are currently living in.

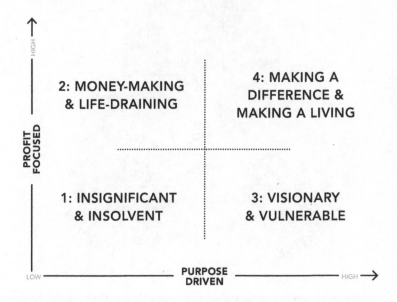

STEP 3: LEVERAGE

Regardless of what quadrant you currently find yourself in, the goal is to spend more and more time in quadrant four. The good news is that there are practical things you can do to gain the positive results of *both* profit *and* purpose so you can make a living *and* make a difference.

Find Your Sweet Spot

The best way to find healthy tension between profit and purpose is to make sure you have positioned your leadership role in your sweet spot. This means you are at the intersection point of a) what you love to do (your passion), b) what you're good at (your expertise), and c) what people need and are willing to pay for (demand).

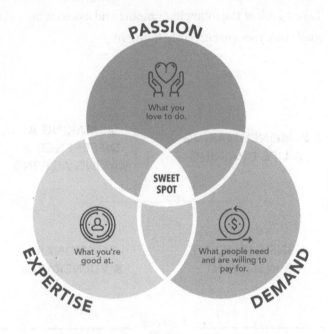

If you are passionate about something that is in high demand, but you are not skilled in that area, you will fail. Our parents tell us as children that we can be anything we want to be if we work hard. That's actually not true. I could endlessly work at improving my hockey skills and it won't allow me to make the NHL; in fact, it won't even allow me to be a good player in a local pickup game. I'm bad at hockey. Period. We need to understand and accept our strengths and weaknesses and live in a way that embraces our strengths.

If you are passionate and skilled about something, but there is no demand for it, then you're likely to be one of the 45% of businesses that fail in their first five years of operation.[3] You'd be wiser to treat that skill as a hobby or bring it to the world in a volunteer capacity.

> *"If the ladder is not leaning against the right wall, every step we take just gets us to the wrong place faster."*
> STEPHEN COVEY

If you are an expert at something that is in high demand, but you are not passionate about it, you're likely to end up as one of the 85% of employees worldwide who are not actively engaged (or are actively disengaged) at work.[4] This means you live a potentially profitable life of passionless work, constantly counting down the days to retirement.

When we have worked hard to constantly position our leadership role in the sweet spot of expertise, passion, and demand, we allow ourselves to tap into the power of healthy tension between profit and purpose.

Create a Dashboard

You would be in a pretty vulnerable and dangerous position if your car didn't have a functional dashboard. Every time you go for a drive, you rely on this dashboard to keep you informed of how fast you're going, how much gas you have, and a variety of other temperatures, pressures, and levels that matter.

Similarly, your business needs a dashboard, and you should be checking this dashboard at least every week. You need accurate, relevant data on *both* profit *and* purpose to keep you informed and to motivate you to continue in the right direction.

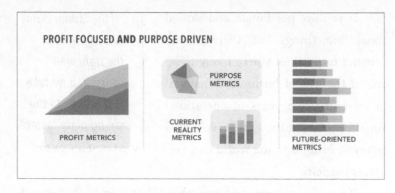

PROFIT FOCUSED **AND** PURPOSE DRIVEN

PROFIT METRICS

PURPOSE METRICS

CURRENT REALITY METRICS

FUTURE-ORIENTED METRICS

Your dashboard should have a few critical elements:

- **Profit Metrics** – Are you making progress toward your financial goals? Are your revenue, expenses, and net income moving in the right direction?

- **Purpose Metrics** – Are you reaching more of your ideal clients? Is the quality and impact of your product or service improving?

- **Current Reality Metrics** – Are you achieving your current goals and objectives? How is your performance on things like production rates, client conversion rates, event attendance, client feedback, or sick days?

- **Future-oriented Metrics** – Are you on track to achieve your future goals and objectives? How is your performance on things like number of blog articles published, percentage of hours dedicated to sales and marketing, or levels of staff training and development?

Your dashboard should be something that you're constantly keeping up to date and reviewing. It should be part of your team meetings, your one-on-one conversations with staff, and your strategy development.

Developing and maintaining an effective dashboard takes time and patience as it will be a continual work in progress. However, once you have a proper dashboard in place and are disciplined to keep it updated, the information will be game changing. It will give you (and your team) the insight to know if you are winning or losing in terms of *both* profit *and* purpose, and the confidence to know what to do next.

AND LEADERSHIP IN ACTION
Colin McAllister and Justin Ryan (a.k.a. The Design Duo)

As interior designers, best-selling authors, and celebrity lifestyle gurus, Colin and Justin love to share good things with good people. The Scottish stars are hosts of many recognizable television shows, including HGTV's *Colin & Justin's Home Heist* and BBC's *The Million Pound Property Experiment*, and their programs are syndicated in countless countries worldwide.

From sofas, chairs, and tables to artwork, lamps, storage, and bedding, their Colin & Justin Home product line is sold internationally in stores such as Winners, Marshalls, and TJ Maxx. They regularly appear as red-carpet hosts, interviewing A-list celebrities such as Madonna, George Clooney, and Bradley Cooper. They have three bestselling books to their credit and are columnists for a long list of publications including *The Toronto Sun*, *The Huffington Post*, and Postmedia properties across Canada.

With so many balls in the air at one time, you might wonder how they keep their eye on the bottom line while, at the same time, ensuring everything they do is aligned with their vision. Interestingly enough, they do both of these things better than anyone I know!

Action Steps

What are things you do to gain the positive results of being profit focused?

- **Make sure plates are spinning other plates.**
  If you look at our business model, we have a lot of spinning plates: products, publishing, TV, real estate, and more. However, we only choose plates that we know will help spin the other plates. As you grow and innovate, you need metrics that prove how each new thing is helping to increase the success of the existing products and services as opposed to stealing time and money away from your core. If the new thing doesn't increase the success of the other things, stop doing it!

- **Know who "your person" is.** Your business will never thrive when you're trying to reach everyone. You have to know "the person" that represents the bullseye of your company and then market, sell, and serve this person in a laser-focused way. Because our person is looking for affordable everyday luxuries, a quality and stylish Colin & Justin mug will be priced at $8, even though we are presented with opportunities that would allow us to sell mugs for $50. This person dictates what stores we're in, what magazines we write for, what TV shows we host, and guides our sales and marketing strategies. Staying focused on this person also makes it easier to say no, even to huge opportunities.

- **Check your blind spots.** Information is power. You need systems in place that keep you critically aware of other people in your space and what they're up to. Which competitors are at your heels? What are they offering? What trends are your customers paying attention to? This information pushes you to reinvent yourself and not get left behind.

What are things you do to gain the positive results of being purpose driven?

- **Know what "your sentence" is.** You need to bring communication clarity to the passion that drives your business. It needs to be one simple sentence or phrase. For us, that phrase is "sharing good things with good people." Based on this, we only say yes to things that align accordingly. These things can be as diverse as selling lamps or hosting a TV show, but they have to fit.

- **Factor in fun.** Our projects are normally stressful, risky, and very demanding, but they are *always* fun. Before we agree to take on anything, from a cottage flip to a magazine interview, we make sure the project allows space for fun and enjoyment. The goal is not all work and no play, it's all work and all play!

- **Be inspiring.** To paraphrase Chesterton, never get bored by never being boring. We start every morning planning how fun and enjoyment will be the arrow that pierces through our day. We take risks often. We decided that our lives will not be about treading the water of our comfort zones, but instead, they'll be about choosing to move out and swim in the big water.

Red Flags

What is an early warning sign that you're overfocusing on profit to the neglect of purpose?

- **A Scent of Stagnation** – Every day, we have the rare privilege to do what we love and what we're good at. A huge red flag to us is anytime we notice that a project is feeling a bit boring or lacks the fun and energy we're accustomed to. We immediately give time and attention to those feelings and try to understand where they're coming from. Is it time for a change? Have we been too comfortable? Are there people we need to be working with more or people we need to be working with less? Is there something we can do to reinvigorate the passion and purpose?

What is an early warning sign that you're overfocusing on purpose to the neglect of profit?

- **Fooled by Fantasy** – As designers, authors, and artists, our work allows us to live in the world of fun and fantasy. However, a cup of fantasy always needs a spoonful of reality. When we recognize that we're overly excited about a new product or service—something that has become a bit of a passion project—we put extra structures and measures in place that will let us know if it's actually delivering and improving our bottom line or not. Just because something is fun and exciting doesn't mean we should be doing it, so we need data that will push us to make hard decisions when necessary.

When Money Matters, Part 2

Let's go back to the dilemma I was facing at the homeless shelter where I questioned if it was possible to live out our vision and pay the bills without begging, borrowing, or stealing. It turned out there was a way, and that turned out to be The Southridge Jam Company.

The shelter was located in an area of Canada that is well known for its tender fruit industry. We learned that a lot of the locally grown peaches, grapes, cherries, and strawberries were left on the ground to rot because they were cosmetically imperfect. A bump, bruise, or unappealing size was all it took to become what's known as a "second." We decided to partner with local farmers and re-purpose their seconds into delicious jam.

Our Southridge Jam team included people who had recently experienced homelessness and were just getting on their feet. This allowed them to gain job skills and experience to build their résumés, and surround themselves with a supportive community of friends to propel them forward into the next chapter of their lives.

We initially hoped to produce and sell a few hundred jars. Within a few short years, we were selling tens of thousands of jars. Today, our small-batch, handcrafted jams are sold online as well as at local businesses, craft shows, and seasonal markets throughout the province. And people know that when they buy our jam, they're not only buying a delicious product, but they are also helping to disrupt the cycle of homelessness, one jar of jam at a time.

The Southridge Jam Company helped us to realize that *both* purpose *and* profit go incredibly well together. In fact, the combination is the very best way to make a living *and* make a difference.

ADDITIONAL RESOURCES

- Book – *Start with Why* by Simon Sinek

- Book – *Essentialism* by Greg McKeown

- Book – *Profit First: A Simple System to Transform Any Business from a Cash-Eating Monster to a Money-Making Machine* by Mike Michalowicz

THE HIGH-PERFORMANCE PARADOX

Having Expectations AND Extending Grace

EXPECTATIONS – *Commitment to goals and targets. Pushing forward despite challenges. Striving for continual improvement.*

GRACE – *Understanding and empathy. Extending forgiveness. Unconditional acceptance.*

The Last Straw? Part 1

When leading the homeless shelter, our team tried to be mindful of the tension between expectations and grace on a daily basis. We had clear house rules that felt helpful and appropriate for everyone to abide by if they chose to reside in our facility. These expectations were around things like refraining from using foul or threatening language, keeping certain areas of the building quiet so people could sleep, and pitching in with some basic chores to help keep the shelter clean.

We also knew there was truth in the words of author Brad Meltzer who wisely said, "Everyone you meet is fighting a battle you know nothing about." Many of the folks who stayed in our shelter had experienced a life of pain, abuse, and loneliness. Beyond this, addictions and mental health challenges often made it impossible for some of our residents to live up to "normal" expectations. They needed a disproportionate level of under-standing and grace.

Every now and then, however, I struggled to extend grace. This happened when a person would come to stay at the shelter and seemed to intentionally cause nothing but trouble. And it didn't feel like this was rooted in a lack of ability to make good decisions; it seemingly came from a lack of caring.

One person in particular who comes to mind is Joey (not his actual name); he proved to be my biggest grace challenge. We would often see Joey stay with us a number of times each year, and every time when he left (which was often due to a suspension), he had caused some form of chaos and confusion in our shelter community. This ranged from agitating other residents until they snapped and got into trouble, to contributing to relapses back into drug or alcohol use for residents who had been doing well in their journey of recovery. He never seemed to leave quietly; he always took people down with him.

After a few years of this, I had reached my breaking point. Although our shelter guidelines stated that people would always be welcomed back—even after a series of suspensions as long as they were not a physical threat to themselves or others—I was ready to throw this guideline out the window. I advocated that continuing to extend grace to Joey would harm the greater good of our community. I suggested something that we had never implemented before: a lifetime ban.

We knew that this was a significant decision for us to make. Was there a point where someone could use up all of their "grace points" and, as a result, have to deal with the reality of hard expectations? Or were we being too hard on Joey? Knowing that we were the one community he could always rely on, were we about to make a decision that could send him down a dark and dangerous road?

STEP 1: UNDERSTAND

Most of us think a person is *either* a driven, type-A sort who is all about relentlessly pushing herself and others toward high expectations, *or* a person is more of an understanding, relational type who is easy going with people and supports them regardless of their successes or failures. Successful leaders, however, know the real magic of high performance is to embrace *both*, setting high expectations while extending just as high levels of grace.

Great Expectations

Andrew Carnegie said, "If you want to be happy, set a goal that commands your thoughts, liberates your energy, and inspires your hopes," and I resonate strongly with these words. Whether I'm working on a new book, trying to level-up my business, learning a new skill, or trying to stay healthy, pushing myself through goals, targets, and timelines often leads to personal success. I have tried to live my life in a way that places high expectations on what I do and how I do it so I'm able to tap into my full potential and impact the world in the greatest possible way.

And this applies to others as well. Stephen R. Covey was onto something when he said, "Treat a person as they are, and they will remain as they are. Treat a person as they can and should be, and they will become as they can and should be." Whether I'm mentoring a team member, challenging a friend to be their best, coaching my son's hockey team, or trying to be a responsible parent, my job is to see the very best in people—even when they don't see it in themselves—and call this out of them.

I can think of a handful of people who took this role in my life—leaders, mentors, and teachers who I looked up to and who didn't let me settle for less than my very best. I didn't always like it at the time, but now I can look back and see how their high expectations pushed me to be a better version of myself, better than I thought I was capable of.

Amazing Grace

You could read all of these wonderful quotes from Carnegie and Covey and conclude that expectations are where it's at. At the end of the day, if you want to experience peak performance, relentlessly push yourself and others to achieve their full potential. Yet, I think there's just as much wisdom in the words of novelist Anne Lamott who wrote, "Expectations are resentments under construction." If all I'm about is high personal expectations and constantly pushing myself to the next level, I'll never be truly satisfied and happy with the present. And if I'm pushing others in the same way, they'll realize that they will never be able to please me or feel they've 'met the mark.'

So, what is the best path to high performance? Are high expectations what it takes to tap into the true potential of yourself and others, or does an environment of grace and acceptance provide the safety and freedom people need to uncover their very best?

The answer, of course, is...YES!

Supportive and Striving

The tension between expectations and grace is the most difficult tension for me to manage personally. I have a strong bias toward expectations and can easily find myself living in the downside of this value. So, as much as I've written this chapter for you, I have written it just as much for myself.

When I have had high yet healthy expectations of those around me, I have seen how this can help people break down the walls of their comfort zone and tap into their true potential. I have also learned—both in working relationships and as a parent and a husband—that expectations without grace never help. They result in resentment, frustration, and the weakening of relationship.

Although it's important to have expectations and grace for those around me, it's just as important (or even more so) to have high levels of expectations and grace for myself.

I am also constantly reminded of the fact that although it's important to have expectations and grace for those around me, it's just as important (or even more so) to have high levels of expectations and grace for myself. I am only able to tap into the best version of myself when I am able to take an AND approach to leadership and hold these two values in healthy tension.

Healthy Tension?

By now, it should be clear that finding healthy tension between expectations and grace is critical to leadership resilience and results. As the graphic below illustrates, there are positive results that can only come from having expectations and extending grace; and there are negative results that are inevitable if you overdo one side to the neglect of the other.

TENSION

Having Expectations and Extending Grace

<table>
<tr>
<td>

+ POSITIVE RESULTS OF EXPECTATIONS

- People constantly stretch their skills and abilities
- Continual improvements and high accountability
- Creates a results-oriented culture

</td>
<td>

POSITIVE RESULTS OF GRACE +

- Unique circumstances are considered
- Provides freedom to take risks and try new things
- Creates a trusting and empathetic culture

</td>
</tr>
</table>

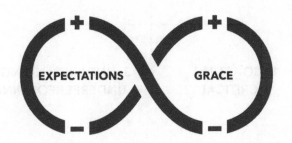

<table>
<tr>
<td>

− NEGATIVE RESULTS WHEN OVERDONE

- People feel they are only valued for their productivity
- Staff "play it safe" due to fear of making mistakes
- Creates a culture of burnout and stress

</td>
<td>

NEGATIVE RESULTS WHEN OVERDONE −

- People fail to tap into their very best
- Mistakes and missed opportunities impact performance
- Creates a culture of mediocrity and low accountability

</td>
</tr>
</table>

STEP 2: ASSESS

Reflect on your thoughts and actions this past season. Have you had high and healthy expectations of yourself and those around you? At the same time, have you been understanding and embraced a high level of grace? Take a look at the following graphic and assess which of the four quadrants you are currently living in.

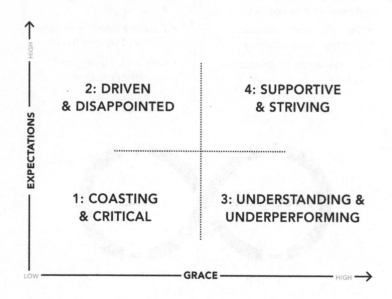

STEP 3: LEVERAGE

Regardless of what quadrant you currently find yourself in, the goal is to spend more and more time in quadrant four. The good news is that there are practical things you can do to gain the positive results of *both* expectations *and* grace so your leadership will be known as supportive and striving.

Comfort Zones

Early in my career, I did a lot of my leadership development work in the field of outdoor experiential education. This often had me taking participants to high-ropes courses, getting them to harness up, and then challenging them to climb up the telephone poles and tackle a variety of challenges once they reached the top. There were lots of ways I integrated leadership development into these experiences; however, the biggest application was the ability for people to understand the concept of comfort zones and explore what it took to move beyond them.

There are many models and theories that point to this concept of comfort zones. Generally, they suggest that, as humans, we have three zones to be aware of:

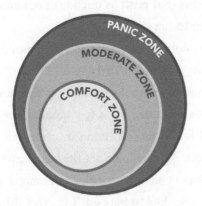

- **Comfort Zone –** A safe place you're comfortable, confident, and familiar with; doesn't take a lot of physical, emotional, or mental energy

- **Moderate Zone –** A place where you are being stretched physically, emotionally, or mentally; also known as your learning zone

- **Panic Zone –** An unhealthy place that often results in one of three primal reactions: fight, flight, or freeze; also known as your shut-down zone

> *"The greatest danger for most of us is not that our aim is too high, and we miss it, but that it is too low, and we reach it."*
>
> MICHELANGELO

There are a few things about comfort zones that have a direct and important connection to setting healthy expectations. Leadership development expert Michael Hyatt wisely said, "The most interesting things in life happen just on the other side of your comfort zone." I think what he was getting at is, although spending time in our comfort zone is important—we can be confident in our skills, be efficient, and, at times, recharge in this safe and familiar place—too much time here results in apathy, stagnation, and fear of the unknown. Positive change in our lives, learning, and growth will only come from having expectations that push us outside of our comfort zone and into the moderate zone.

Interestingly enough, by doing this, we are able to move new things into our comfort zones over time. Early into COVID-19, I had to learn a ton of new online technologies and platforms in order to deliver our programs virtually. For a few months, there wasn't a single day where I found myself living in my comfort zone, and it wasn't always fun. But our team set the clear expectation of being industry leaders in effective virtual workshops, so moving outside my comfort zone had to happen. The great thing was that, within a few months, all these new virtual challenges had become familiar; I had moved them into my comfort zone.

It's also important to note that although healthy expectations will push us (and others) outside of comfort zones, the trick is to ensure we're not moving into the panic zone. Positive results rarely come from being in this shut-down zone because we've gone from being challenged to being afraid. Leaders need to ensure their expectations are set firmly in the moderate zone, and when challenging others, they should make sure they're not pushing people into the panic zone.

Be Challenging AND Realistic

It is also important to make sure that, at any given time, you are only moving outside your comfort zone in a few important, calculated ways. You need to have ample time in your comfort zone; this is where you recharge, feel your best, and deliver results. If your expectations are pushing you outside your comfort zone in a long list of ways, you're setting yourself up for failure. Instead of moving into your moderate zone in eight or nine different ways, move there in two or three ways at any given time.

This can be easier said than done. My personality type is often referred to as "assertive-directive," and I'm an Enneagram 3, which means my sense of self-worth can come through achievement. If I'm not careful, I can have about a dozen exciting change initiatives happening at work while trying to pick up a new language, write a book, and learn to make bread at home. The problem is that when I'm unrealistic with the number of things that have me outside of my comfort zone, none of them work out. I become overwhelmed, burnt out, and quite unpleasant to be around.

I've learned that there should be no more than three expectations in my life at any given time that take me outside of my comfort zone, and I check in on this each week. Normally, I plan for each expectation to be a three-month goal. Until I have achieved these goals, I discipline myself not to add more stretch goals to the list, as these will become unrealistic, unhelpful expectations.

The same is true of expectations on others. If you're leading a team, be clear on the number of things that have the team and each individual outside their comfort zones. Ensure your expectations are challenging and pushing them in a healthy way but at the same time are realistic and setting them up for success. Also, check in with people to see if they have what they need to succeed within their moderate zone so they don't get pushed into their panic zone.

Choose Generosity

I used to think that choosing generosity meant volunteering your time or giving money to charity; however, I've come to realize that this is a very limited perspective. In fact, the most powerful way we can choose generosity is through our assumptions about others. You've been leading long enough to know that people won't always live up to your expectations. When this happens, you have a choice. You can choose to assume the worst (i.e., they don't care, they don't have what it takes, they are against me, etc.), or you can choose generosity and make the least negative assumption (i.e., they were trying their best, something might be holding them back, I may have been unrealistic, etc.).

In her book, *Dare to Lead*,[1] Dr. Brené Brown teaches that choosing generosity means we extend the most generous interpretation to the intent, words, and actions of others. This means that we assume people are always doing their best—always—even when they let us down, even when they do hurtful, bad, or downright unwise things. You make the deliberate choice to assume positive intent until you are proved wrong, which, based on my experience, happens very rarely.

One practical way our team at the homeless shelter tried to apply this concept in our day-to-day work was by disciplining ourselves to stop using the phrase, "What is wrong with that person?" and replace it with, "What might have happened to that person?" This sounds simple, yet it had profound impact on how we viewed a person or interpreted why they hadn't met our expectations. It opened the door for grace, empathy, and understanding.

> *"I know my life is better when I work from the assumption that everyone is doing the best they can."*
> BRENÉ BROWN

The paradoxical benefit in all of this is that when you extend grace to someone by choosing generosity, you win as well.

When you're a leader who chooses generosity, even in the rare event that you're wrong (and the person did have negative intent), you'll find you're a happier, more positive person overall. Choosing generosity is choosing positivity over negativity, optimism over pessimism, and faith in humanity over distrust in humanity. Over time, this has positive impact on your energy, general mood, and even mental health.

It's also important to note that we need to choose generosity with ourselves sometimes. As leaders, we will not always live up to our own high expectations. Practise assuming the best about yourself at these times instead of the worst. Extending grace to ourselves allows us to extend it to others.

Give Permission Slips

Another powerful way to increase your level of grace also comes from *Dare to Lead* where Dr. Brown talks about the concept of "permission slips." This goes back to elementary school when you needed a signed piece of paper that would extend to you permission to leave class for a field trip or compete in a sporting event. What's noteworthy is that our need for permission slips doesn't end when we finish school; in fact, as a leader, giving permission slips to ourselves and to others is more important than ever.

For example, in the first few months of COVID-19, our team had to shift all of our speaking and training from in-person to online delivery. During that time, I gave the team permission slips that allowed them to be beginners. This extended them grace to make some mistakes. I actually wrote these permission slips on Post-it Notes and told the team to stick them on their desks for a month so they wouldn't forget.

During that same season, my wife and I were trying to deliver on work commitments while unexpectedly homeschooling our kids due to COVID-19 lockdowns. We gave each other permission slips to have a less tidy house and to eat takeout a little more often than we normally do. These permission slips were only valid for a little while but long enough to get through the season without feeling the heaviness and guilt of unmet expectations.

It's important to note that giving out a permission slip doesn't mean you no longer have high expectations. It's just a short-term allowance of grace that accounts for the fact that "life happens."

AND LEADERSHIP IN ACTION
Chandra Irvin

Chandra is the executive director of the Center for Peace and Spiritual Renewal at Spalding University in Louisville, Kentucky. She also serves on Spalding's leadership team to help create and implement institutional strategies that promote peace and justice within and beyond the Spalding community.

As author of the book, *Do You See What I See?: A Diversity Tale for Retaining People of Color*,[2] and founder and president of Irvin, Goforth & Irvin LLC, Chandra consults with leaders from across the world, helping them build strategies that improve relationships and performance in diverse environments.

When working on this chapter, Chandra was the first person who came to mind to interview. Over the past decade, I've had the privilege of working with, learning from, and being friends with this incredible woman, and I feel that she embodies the heathy tension between expectations and grace better than anyone I know.

Action Steps

What are things you do to gain the positive results of expectations?

- **Respect the rubric.** When I was a student, I was confident that I could get an A as long as I had a rubric to work with. The rubric provided a scoring guide that my work would be measured against and was explicit in describing the professor's performance expectations. Without it, I was just guessing on the measure of success.

  As leaders, we need to have a rubric of our expectations so there is clarity on what success looks like and how it will be measured. Otherwise, you end up lost in a world of confusion, constantly wondering if you are measuring up or not.

- **Treat expectations like a team sport.** As a leader, when you have expectations on others, it's critical that you involve them in developing the plan for how these expectations will be met. Start by making sure the expectations are in fact clear. Then, explore how these expectations can become a reality in ways that tap into the natural energy, skills, strengths, and values of those you lead. Without their input and buy-in, they'll either fail to deliver, or you'll end up draining and disengaging them with your one-size-fits-all approach.

What are things you do to gain the positive results of grace?

- **Start with self.** If you are not able to extend grace to yourself or receive it when it's given to you, you will not be able to offer it to others. This means that you must accept and embrace your humanity, *both* the imperfections of it *and* the beauty of it. You recognize and are comfortable with the true value that lies within yourself, regardless of what you do or don't do. This is not performance based; it's who you are at your core—the natural light that is within you. If you are not in touch with this light or don't believe in it, it will be impossible for you to see it in others.

- **Dig deep.** Even when you've extended grace to yourself and are able to extend it to others, there will always be people in your life who will really test your limits. These people won't even come close to meeting your expectations or will do harmful, hurtful, and irresponsible things. It is *still* important to extend grace to these people. This doesn't mean you agree with them or support their views, it simply means that you believe every person on the planet has the same light inside them that you do, and you're responsible to seek it—even if it's just a tiny spark.

Think of the times in your life when you've been extended grace that wasn't deserved, times when you messed up and still had someone by your side. Then see yourself in that person you now find difficult and realize that, like you, they need grace, too. In fact, grace might be their only hope.

Red Flags

What are early warning signs that you're overfocusing on expectations to the neglect of grace?

- **The Light Goes Out** – When I realize that it's hard for me to muster up any grace towards a person whatsoever, and my only feelings towards them are negative and dark, that's a sign that I need to step back and re-evaluate things. It's normally an indicator that my drive to achieve results and have my expectations met based on my values, beliefs, and goals have overpowered my ability to see the spark of humanity and light in people who let me down or don't live according to these values. It's often the people who I struggle and disagree with the most that provide me the biggest opportunities to tap into the power of grace in my life if I choose to go there.

- **Poor Listening** – I have found that I tend to be neglecting grace, empathy, and understanding when, instead of listening, I find myself drifting into what Cari Jackson[3] calls "lethal listening styles." I can tell this is happening if I'm:

  - Analyzing what the other person is saying when I should just listen to understand what they are experiencing.

  - Coopting the conversation by shifting from their agenda to my own.

  - Allowing my mind to drift as the other person is speaking.

  - Assuming I know where the other person is going in the conversation before they finish.

  - Thinking of quick fixes that might help the person resolve their concerns.

What are early warning signs that you're overfocusing on grace to the neglect of expectations?

- **Permanent Vacation** – If you live a life with high expectations, having breaks is important. As a leader, if you don't give yourself these breaks to recover and recharge, you'll have less to give others and the light within you will dim. However, it's important to recognize the difference between recovery and complacency. For example, when I'm taking a breather in my lifelong work that fights for equity, inclusion, and belonging, I have to make sure I'm not saying to myself, "Let someone else do it." If someone says to me, "I haven't seen you do much lately; are you walking your talk?," it's important to know that I can honestly say, "Yes."

- **Unclear Expectations** – When expectations are so nebulous or vague that you can't specifically artic- ulate what you're responsible for or contributing to, you're fooling yourself. No one person should ever be fully responsible, but every person has a role to play and should be clear on what success looks like.

The Last Straw? Part 2

Let's go back to my opening story when I was close to issuing the first lifetime ban at the homeless shelter. Fast forward about seven years after being at the crossroads with Joey. I'm driving into the entrance of our local university looking for a parking spot so I can attend a special event. Parking is hard to find, but once I find a spot and make my way to the main auditorium, I see that the place is packed with a line out the door.

The special event was an educational one focused on the Sixties Scoop, a mass removal of Indigenous children from their families and subsequent placement into the child welfare sys- tem in Canada. It's called the Sixties Scoop because the highest number of these "adoptions" took place in the 1960s, and because, in many instances, children were literally scooped from their homes and communities without the knowledge or consent of their families.

With the goal of "taking the Indian out of them," children of the Sixties Scoop were raised without any connection to their First Nations identity. Not surprisingly, many of these children went on to experience psychological and emotional problems later in life when they learned about their birth families and Aboriginal heritage.[4] This often resulted in addictions, mental health challenges, and even homelessness.

Although I didn't know it when he was staying in our shelter, it turned out that Joey was a child of the Sixties Scoop.

What is important to understand about this event is that it wasn't merely a chance for me to learn about an oppressive system that had had a negative, long-term impact on Joey; I was actually invited as a guest by the founder and host of the event who happened to be none other than Joey.

You see, in the years since deciding whether we were going to give Joey a lifetime ban—which thankfully we decided not to do—Joey had turned his life around completely. He worked hard to get off the street and secure housing, and then, he obtained his high-school equivalency, which allowed him to apply to university. He went on to graduate with a degree in Aboriginal Education and to dedicate his life to helping others who, like himself, were victims of the Sixties Scoop. He truly had become a local hero.

During the event, I looked at Joey and on numerous occasions had to wipe tears from my eyes. I was so thankful we hadn't made the decision to give up on Joey and stop extending him grace. I was also thankful for the high expectations we continued to hold him to that pushed him to make better decisions. Mostly, I was grateful for the high expectations he held himself to that led him to have so much positive impact on the world.

I vowed that day that no matter how much a person upsets me or how much I may disagree with their views or behaviours, I would never stop having grace for them. I would never play a role in limiting the potential of a person like Joey. I also find that when I'm really struggling to have grace with someone, I think of Joey and remember that sometimes the most challenging people possess the greatest ability to change the world if they're given the gift of high expectations and high levels of grace.

ADDITIONAL RESOURCES

- Book – *Dare to Lead* by Brené Brown

CHAPTER 7

ALL IN BUT BURNT OUT

Caring for Others AND Caring for Yourself

CARE FOR SELF – *Prioritizing time to maintain or improve your own mental, physical, emotional, and spiritual health. Focusing on yourself.*

CARE FOR OTHERS – *Reaching out to make a difference in the lives of your friends, family, and community. Living beyond yourself.*

A Bad Plan, Part 1

The year 2007 was proving to be quite a year. I had just sold my leadership development company to take on a new job at the homeless shelter. I was trying to be a supportive son as my dad journeyed through cancer treatment. After a few amazing years of dating and getting to know one another, Becky and I walked down the aisle and became husband and wife. And, oh yeah, we had someone without a home living in ours.

I entered into the year overwhelmed with gratitude. I realized how incredibly fortunate I was to have the sale of my business provide me with the luxury of starting my new lower-paying role without financial concerns. Serving in the shelter every day and seeing the pain, stigmatization, and health challenges so many of my street-involved friends faced made me realize how blessed I was to have the health, connections, and community that I often took for granted. My father was responding well to his treatment and was given a very positive prognosis. And I was marrying the most amazing partner imaginable. Life was really, *really* good.

With the belief that "to whom much is given, much is required," I felt a deep sense of responsibility to now live my life with an others-first orientation. I had been blessed in order to be a blessing to others. This meant that my time, talent, and treasure were going to be used to make a difference.

By the beginning of 2008, however, this time/treasure/talent plan wasn't working out so well. When it came to offering up my time to serve others, I found there was simply never enough. The needs in the shelter were overwhelming, and this meant long days (and often nights) being on-call 24/7. With talent in the area of leadership development, I offered my services on the side at no charge to other shelters across the country, but I found that this ended up taking up most of my weekends. And although we were sharing our treasure by providing a room to a friend who was transitioning out of the shelter, it turned out to be a very bad first-year-of-marriage decision, which resulted in some unexpected, big challenges for our relationship.

I was discouraged and burnt out. Was it time to stop prioritizing the needs of others and start to take care of myself? Was I naïve to think that living a life with an others orientation was the right path for me?

STEP 1: UNDERSTAND

Most people think that they have to make a choice between living a life that "looks out for number one" or embraces an approach of "service before self" instead. Successful leaders, however, know that the secret to sustainability is to *both* care for self *and* care for others.

Is It Me or Is It You?

Our consumeristic culture works hard to convince us that in order to be happy, we simply need more. More stuff. More entertainment. More money. Eat, drink, and be merry! Yet I believe that most people at their core resonate with a different point of view, one powerfully described by author and researcher Daniel Goleman[1]:

> "Self-absorption in all its forms kills empathy, let alone compassion. When we focus on ourselves, our world contracts as our problems and preoccupations loom large. But when we focus on others, our world expands. Our own problems drift to the periphery of the mind and so seem smaller, and we increase our capacity for connection—or compassionate action."

Goleman is suggesting that the real secret to happiness is deliberately choosing to have less so others can have more. It's using our time, talent, and treasure to make a difference in the lives of our family, friends, community, and, specifically, those in need. When the weight of the world is heavy on our shoulders, perhaps the best way to get out of our own head is to simply focus on the needs of others.

I think most people believe that to whom much is given, much is required, and they want to live a life that steps up to this responsibility. As I stated in the first chapter of this book, I saw this innate desire to serve others lived out almost every day when I worked in the homeless shelter. People would email me or come to our building looking for volunteering opportunities. Cars would drive up to our facility each day to drop off donations of food, clothing, and finances. Companies would reach out to us wanting to explore ways they could partner with us to help serve our homeless friends. Most people wanted to make a difference.

This difference-making aspiration is particularly true in the lives of leaders—people like you who choose to work long hours and take on difficult challenges to serve your clients, your teams, and the companies you work for.

Why, then, do so few people stick with their efforts to make a difference? The harsh reality is that making a difference often comes with a high personal cost. Sadly, when you look beneath the surface of some of the most incredible difference-makers in recent history, you'll often find family breakdowns, health issues, depression, and burnout. Their commitment to others was all-consuming and left them running on empty. It makes you question if it's possible to lay down your life *and* have a life?

Because of this reality, many people suppress their desire to serve others and instead focus on developing themselves. Championing the slogan, "If you don't take care of yourself, no one else will," the self-help industry will claim a market size of over $13 billion dollars the year I'm writing this book,[2] and will grow approximately 5% the following year. This includes books, courses, coaching, podcasts, and motivational speakers all providing personal effectiveness solutions aimed at guiding you to long-term happiness.

The industry is clear that you need to wisely invest your hard-earned money to secure the fun and safe early retirement you deserve, you need to prioritize your daily productivity rituals over the needless interruptions and annoying needs of others, and you need to tap into your personal power instead of letting other people's needs or drama bring you down.

Obviously, investing in your own well-being and personal development is not a bad thing. It's critical. There is wisdom in the words of mental health advocate Katie Reed who said, "Self-care is giving the world the best of you, instead of what's left of you." But like many things in life, there can be too much of a good thing.

Out of the friends and colleagues who I watched go "all-in" with this self-improvement approach,

Caring for others and caring for yourself is possibly the most mismanaged tension in our world right now.

I've seen very, very few of them grow in sustained happiness or fulfillment. Unfortunately, the ones who seemed to be flying to every self-help conference in the world and enrolling in countless coaching programs and mastermind groups struggled the most. I watched their marriages fall apart, their careers get off track, and their overall well-being deteriorate.

So, if living your life completely focused on the needs of others is a one-way path to burnout while living your life completely focused on your own needs will ultimately rob you of fulfillment or impact, is there a secret to caring for others while not neglecting yourself in the process?

The Secret to Sustainability

I feel that out of the six tensions this book focuses on, caring for others and caring for yourself is possibly the most mismanaged tension in our world right now. This is not only true in the lives of leaders but in the lives of everyone. People are often at one extreme or the other. Is this true for you when you're around your friends, family, and coworkers?

Uncovering the secret that caring for self and caring for others is not a problem to solve but rather a tension to manage is game changing. Once you realize that you don't have to pick a side, and that true impact, happiness, and fulfillment come from taking an AND approach, your world—and the world around you—becomes a better place.

Healthy Tension?

By now, it should be clear that finding healthy tension between care for self and care for others is critical to leadership resilience and results. As the graphic below illustrates, there are positive results that can only come from embracing *both* caring for self *and* others; and there are inevitable negative results if you overdo one side to the neglect of the other.

TENSION
Caring for Others and Caring for Yourself

POSITIVE RESULTS OF CARING FOR YOURSELF

- Stay grounded, present, and peaceful
- Acknowledge your unique needs
- Have the energy and attitude needed to serve others well

POSITIVE RESULTS OF CARING FOR OTHERS

- Make a difference in the lives of those in need
- Less focus on your problems by focusing on the needs of others
- Develop gratitude and a feeling of contribution

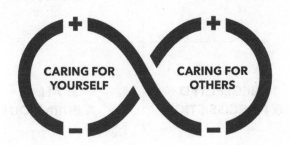

CARING FOR YOURSELF

CARING FOR OTHERS

NEGATIVE RESULTS WHEN OVERDONE

- Have little impact on the world around you
- Get lost in your own needs and worries
- Develop a sense of entitlement

NEGATIVE RESULTS WHEN OVERDONE

- Lose peace-of-mind and sense of control
- Become frustrated and resentful
- Personal burnout and inability to help anyone

STEP 2: ASSESS

Reflect on your thoughts and actions this past season. Have you prioritized time to care for your own mental, physical, emotional, and spiritual health? Have you deliberately reached out to make a difference to those around you and lived beyond yourself? Take a look at the following graphic and assess which of the four quadrants you are currently living in.

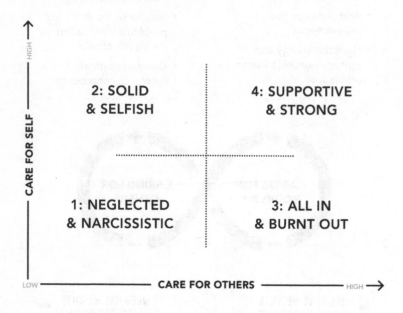

STEP 3: LEVERAGE

Regardless of what quadrant you currently find yourself in, the goal is to spend more and more time in quadrant four. The good news is that there are practical things you can do to gain the positive results of *both* caring for self *and* others, so you become *both* stronger *and* more supportive.

Return on Investment

At the end of the day, managing the tension between self and others in a healthy way will come down to time—how you view your time and how you spend your time.

A good friend of mine once pointed out to me the profound insight that most people treat the resource of their time very differently than the other resources in their lives, such as their possessions or their money. We fiercely guard and protect our money and possessions, yet we freely give away our time as if it were of very little value.

I'd often see this lived out when working in the homeless shelter. I would have wealthy people ask me if it was "a good use of their money" to give a person on the street corner a few dollars. They wanted to be sure that the investment of a few of their hard-earned dollars was a wise one. Yet when it came to their time, I knew that these same people wouldn't think twice about saying yes to a coffee meeting with anyone who asked and would have no issue binging a few hours of Netflix each night.

> *We fiercely guard and protect our money and possessions, yet we freely give away our time as if it were of very little value.*

I've seen it in my own life, too, as I've caught myself doom-scrolling on social media or overcommitting myself to things that really don't matter.

In the book, *The 7 Habits of Highly Effective People*,[3] author Stephen Covey suggests that "the key is not spending time, but investing it." Like your attempt at ensuring the money you're putting away for retirement is getting the best possible return on investment, you need to think about how you can invest your time to get the best possible return as well.

It was over 30 years ago when I first came across the simple yet profound way Dr. Covey suggested I look at how I spend my time. In what he refers to as the Time Management Matrix (also known as the Eisenhower Matrix), Covey shows that everything a person does in a day will fall into one of four quadrants. This model is so old it's almost new, but in our ultra-connected and over-programmed world, I think it's probably more relevant today than it's ever been.

THE 4 QUADRANTS OF TIME

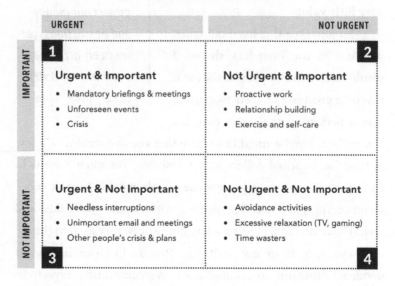

Thanks to Stephen R. Covey, The 7 Habits of Highly Effective People

Using the criteria of urgency (i.e., things that need to be done right away) and importance (i.e., things that are a wise use of time), you can place everything you do throughout the day in one of the four quadrants.

Covey's big idea is that the most effective people in life are always looking for ways to steal time from quadrants 1, 3, and 4, and shift that time into quadrant 2. This often comes from:

- Reducing or eliminating time wasters from quadrant 4 (e.g., putting a time limit on your TV watching or taking social media apps off your phone).

- Delegating or declining things in quadrant 3 by realizing it's OK to say no.

- Doing things from quadrant 1 right away so you can check them off your list.

When it comes to finding healthy tension between self and others, you will need to find a way to spend more time in the non-urgent but important space of quadrant 2 for either self-care (e.g., exercise, sleep, hobbies, etc.) or difference-making (e.g., volunteering, reaching out to those in need, etc.).

My encouragement is to start small! Don't feel that you need to suddenly invest two hours a day into taking care of yourself or one day a week into reaching out to others. It will never happen. Look realistically at what it would take to steal 10 to 15 minutes a day from one of the other quadrants and shift that time into caring for self or others.

Once you've succeeded in carving out 10 minutes a day or one hour a week, ask yourself, "What is going to give me the biggest return on investment?" The answer is going to be different for everyone, but whatever it is, that's where you should continue to focus.

Care for Others – Three Key Questions

If you plan to use the newfound time to make a difference in the lives of others, start by asking yourself three important questions: What do I care about? What am I good at? What is an easy way to integrate these two things?

What do I care about? All of us are both naturally wired and nurtured over time to have certain things we deeply care about, things like injustices that keep us up at night or break our hearts. For some, it's homelessness. For others, it's animal welfare. For still others, it's climate change.

What do you care about? It's important that you're clear on this, because if you can be strategic in making sure the time you invest to care for others is in this area, you'll look forward to every time you engage in a related activity, and you'll feel that you're truly making a difference.

What am I good at? Everyone has unique skills and talents. Maybe you're great at cooking or building things or creating websites or simply being a good listener. Regardless of what your skills are, look for ways to use these natural abilities to make a difference in the lives of others. Not only will this be an enjoyable way for you to give back, but it will also be the way you will have the most significant impact.

What's an easy way to integrate these two things? Don't fool yourself into thinking that you need to get on a plane and travel to a war-torn country to make a difference. I am 100% convinced that no matter who you are or where you live, there are needs you alone can meet in your own neighbourhood: the single parent who needs a night off, the newcomer who has just immigrated and is desperate for someone to help her learn English through friendly conversation, the senior who could really benefit from a visit once a week. If you find an easy, convenient way to make a difference, you are much more likely to do it consistently.

I am 100% convinced that no matter who you are or where you live, there are needs you alone can meet in your own neighbourhood.

Before we continue, I'd like to note that some people reading this book are at full capacity by simply caring for the people who depend on them at work and at home. If this is you, don't allow yourself to feel guilty for not doing more to save the whales, free the children, or cool the planet. There are seasons for everything, and in some seasons of life, the needs of those who depend on us—from young children to aging parents to sick friends—are all we have space to focus on. There will be other seasons where you will have the capacity to reach beyond these needs, but for now, be OK with your focus being on those who need you the most.

Care for Self – Manageable and Meaningful

When talking with my friend and self-care expert Laura Hughes[4] about how to use the time you carve out to invest in yourself, she stresses two important things you need to keep in mind.

First, you must find the unique form of self-care that is most meaningful for you. Each of us has different needs, and part of practising effective self-care is knowing which actions feel most supportive and help you feel the way you want to feel. Don't let marketing, social-media comparison, or celebrity culture convince you that you need a spa day or a Disney vacation. That might not be realistic for you or might not actually fill you up. What is meaningful for you? Is it reading a book, going for a walk, doing a puzzle, calling a loved one, getting outside?

Second, you need to remember that effective self-care needs to be manageable. It's doing simple things consistently that make the biggest impact on your mental wellness and health. Don't beat yourself up for all the things you're not doing! Instead, just start adding simple rituals to your day and to your week, things you know you can commit to and follow through with. Schedule time each day for some stretching or a walk outside. Fill up your water bottle after breakfast and again after lunch, and commit to drinking it fully each time. Set up a daily or weekly phone or video chat with family. Enjoy a cup of tea in a cozy spot before a shift or opening your laptop in the morning.

As you work to find the time—even a small amount of time—to invest in yourself each day, you will gain the strength and peace of mind to serve others well. When you acknowledge and accept your needs and prioritize them as much as the needs of others, your resilience begins to grow.

AND LEADERSHIP IN ACTION
Jason Russell

Jason Russell is a person who truly embodies the value of focusing on others. He is a human-rights activist and filmmaker who co-founded Invisible Children[5] and directed the *KONY 2012* documentary. This film focused on Joseph Kony, the self-appointed "messiah" of the Lord's Resistance Army (LRA) who oversees the rebel group responsible for Africa's longest-running armed conflict. Kony has kidnapped over 30,000 children to strengthen his army, forcing the boys to become soldiers and the girls to become sex slaves.

In many ways, *KONY 2012* was an experiment. Could an online video make an obscure war criminal infamous? And if he was infamous, would the world work together to stop him? The answer was a resounding yes. *KONY 2012* became the fastest-growing viral video of all time and resulted in unprecedented international action to end Africa's longest-running conflict.

Within a week of its March 5, 2012 release date, the film had over 120 million views, was translated into every major language, and was responsible for 60% to 70% of all the world's tweets on Twitter. Jason was being interviewed by the who's who of Hollywood and landed on the covers of *The New York Times* and *Time* magazine.

Fast forward 10 days. On March 15, another video involving Jason went viral, but not in the way he wanted. This iPhone video, purchased and shared by TMZ, showed Jason staggering through the streets of San Diego without clothing and screaming obscenities. The personal toll of overfocusing on others to the neglect of taking care of himself had led to a total mental and emotional breakdown and, ultimately, to hospitalization.

Believing that breakdowns can lead to breakthroughs, and realizing that the pressure he faced associated with *KONY 2012* was unprecedented, Jason refused to be defeated. He bravely chose to move forward and give himself what he needed to be healthy mentally, emotionally, and spiritually. He went on to consult with the Bill & Melinda Gates Foundation, TOMS, charity: water, and International Justice Mission, and continues to support the incredible work of Invisible Children.

For more insight into Jason's world-changing work with Invisible Children, his breakdown, and his courageous recovery, I encourage you to watch Season 2, Episode 213 of *Oprah's Next*

Chapter as more time is given to do justice to the story. What I want to focus on are the powerful things Jason has learned through this journey.

When it comes to managing the tension between self and others in a healthy way, Jason understands how important this is better than any person I know. He has used *both* his successes *and* his failures to provide us with powerful insights on how we can manage this tension wisely.

Action Steps

What are things that you do to gain the positive results of caring for others?

- **Avoid comparisons.** Don't waste your time or energy comparing what you're doing to what other people are doing. We get so distracted by looking at what other people are doing and think we must do what they're doing to measure up. This will always disappoint you. If you're expecting to be the next MLK or Gandhi or Mother Teresa, you're setting yourself up for discouragement. It doesn't matter how much anyone else is changing the world, what matters is how you come alive by doing something you love. Ask yourself the questions, "What am I uniquely good at or have expertise in, and how can I use that to help the world?"

- **Start small.** Start with one small ongoing commitment of doing something you love in a way that makes a difference. Then, once that becomes part of your daily or weekly routine, look at what the next small thing is that you can do. In a culture that's all about having your 15 minutes of fame and getting as many likes as possible on social media, your psyche can become saturated with the belief that you need to be known for the big things you're doing. Don't buy into this! Be OK with becoming an "anonymous extraordinary." Focus on what you're doing every day, because we are what we do every day.

What are things you do to gain the positive results of caring for yourself?

- **Get active.** Find the forms of physical activity that you love and just focus on those things. For me, it's running, yoga, cycling, and surfing, so I'm deliberate about making these things part of my routine; exercise never feels like a boring task but instead something I look forward to. I also know that without weaving these things into my schedule and having some form of accountability, they can easily be the first things that get cut when the day gets busy. That's why, for example, I have an 11 o'clock online yoga class that I do each day with a few buddies. Because it's in my calendar and others expect me to be there, I make it happen.

- **Write it down.** I've been journaling almost every day for many, many years. Getting things out of my head and putting them into words on a page is a healthy form of mindfulness and helps me gain perspective. I write down my problems, heartbreaks, successes, and dreams. I decorate my journals and fill them with much more than just my words. I also include notes from friends, pictures that mean a lot to me, tickets to events, and other things that bring me back to that time. Perspective and context can be a paradigm shift. It can rewrite how you see yourself inside the story your mind is constantly telling you. And it can happen in a moment.

- **Read poetry.** At our greatest, we're all teachers, and the greatest teachers are storytellers, and the greatest storytellers are philosophers, and the greatest philosophers are poets. Poets can take something as profound as what it means to have this human journey and put it into a sentence. And in those sentences are the most incredible messages of wisdom, advice, hope, and healing possible. If you have no idea where to start with poetry, I'd suggest the book that changed my life: *Love Poems from God: Twelve Sacred Voices from the East and West* by Daniel Ladinsky.[6]

Red Flags

What are early warning signs that you're overfocusing on others to the neglect of self?

- **Lack of Sleep** – I've always been the type of person who doesn't require a lot of sleep. All through high school and college, I could get by on two or three hours a night. But I realized that I was truly just getting by. Before my breakdown in 2012, I had gone close to 10 straight days with no REM sleep. There was always another interview to give, another message to post, and another team member to check in with. Sadly, this lack of sleep should have been a huge red flag. Now I pay super close attention to my sleeping patterns as the quality of my sleep is a huge indicator of the quality of my mental and emotional health.

Sleep is the foundation underneath nutrition and exercise. You stop working without it. If you or someone you know is having sustained difficulty sleeping, it's a huge red flag. Everyone I have met who has had a mental break was not sleeping well right before. And if you break, it shatters sharp glass for everyone else around you to pick up.

- **Lack of Community** – If you're in a role where you are giving a ton of yourself to serve others, you need a close-knit community of friends (and probably a therapist) who knows how you're doing at all times. Any time you're struggling mentally, physically, or emotionally and someone in your inner circle is not aware of this, that should be a huge red flag that you are moving in a dangerous direction. You can assess the quality of this inner circle by considering their willingness to call you out on red flags they see in your life and the humility you have in receiving this feedback.

- **Lack of Peace** – We are human beings, not human doings. The hardest lesson I have ever learned is if the people who truly know me love me, that's all that matters. Everyone else can have an opinion, but I have tried my best not to take it personally because they honestly don't know me; it's not worth losing my mind over.

What are early warning signs that you're overfocusing on self to the neglect of others?

- **Playing It Safe** – Our culture has us in a constant state of documenting our lives and showing off on social media for the admiration of our peers. This has us addicted to seeking out quick wins. Beyond this, we often fool ourselves into believing that our peers' social media highlight reel of constant success and victory is their real life, and one that we need to measure up to. Because of this need for a quick win, we have become afraid to try new things that might lead to failure. We play it safe to ensure that we can always show a smiling, successful face to the outside world. But the truth is, most people who have experienced true success in making a difference in the world have failed so many times. And some of the best, most important lessons in our lives will only come through failure.

My breakdown during *KONY 2012* was incredibly hard and I don't wish that trauma, PTSD, fear, or shame on anyone. It was and has been truly terrible.

But I now have empathy for and can relate to people who are hurting in a totally different way. I can genuinely say, "That happened to me, too." And that's the moment the healing comes in. Turns out, we need one another to heal one another, and the ones who've survived the fire have scars to share. If you're playing it safe and not failing now and then, it's probably a red flag you're not trying hard enough or taking enough risks to make a difference.

A Bad Plan, Part 2

Going back to my opening story, within a very short amount of time, it became clear that my plan of living my life with an others orientation was quite flawed. The intent was good, but the impact was proving to be disastrous. At work, my 24/7 commitment level had me burnt out, and sadly, I found that I was starting to resent the very people I was trying to support.

Financially, it was starting to become clear that my decisions were not going to be responsible ones for me or my family in the long term. My house was not a restful home, and the pressures of having a homeless person living with us was taking a toll on my marriage. Something had to change.

Having a mentor in your life is so incredibly important when it comes to managing the tension of self and others as well as all the other tensions in this book.

Thankfully, I had a wonderful mentor in my life at that time, someone who successfully lived out many of my difference-making aspirations but was a few chapters ahead of me in life and had the wisdom of experience. He was able to kindly speak some hard truth into my life and paint a picture of what my life would look like if I continued down the road I was on. It wasn't a pretty picture, and if it hadn't come from him, I don't think I would have been able to see it on my own. Having a mentor in your life is so incredibly important when it comes to managing the tension of self and others as well as all the other tensions in this book.

After the input from my mentor, I decided a few things in my life had to change quickly. The first was to find another suitable living option for our street-involved friend and reclaim our house as a home. The next change was to take advantage of the wonderful work of Dr. Henry Cloud and John S. Townsend around setting boundaries[7] and set some in my life at work and at home. These boundaries focused on things ranging from the number of hours I worked and the amount of time I allowed myself to be on-call, to when and how much I was willing to give financial support to people in need. Setting these boundaries and living them out was hard work but proved to have great benefit.

Some of the changes were longer term. I worked with Becky on developing a new plan for our future, one that was *both* others oriented *and* invested in ourselves. I worked with a counsellor to explore what had led to this self/others tension being so horribly mismanaged, and what I needed to work on within myself to ensure I lived out this new plan for my and Becky's life. I committed to developing some of my interests, like fishing and running, and making them part of my weekly routine.

Over a decade later, managing this tension well is still a work in progress, but I'm pleased to say that things are continuing to move in the right direction as I'm determined to lead the way forward through the power of AND.

ADDITIONAL RESOURCES

- Book – *The 7 Habits of Highly Effective People* by Stephen R. Covey (Habit #3)

- Book – *Love Poems from God: Twelve Sacred Voices from the East and West* by Daniel Ladinsky

- Book – *Boundaries: When to Say Yes, How to Say No to Take Control of Your Life* by Dr. Henry Cloud and Dr. John Townsend

- Video – "Unexpected," Jason Russell, TEDx Talks, https://www.ted.com/watch/tedx-talks

CHAPTER 8

DO I HAVE WHAT IT TAKES?

Building Confidence AND Remaining Humble

CONFIDENCE – *A belief in yourself and your ability to deal with life's challenges. A realistic sense of your capabilities and feeling secure in that knowledge.*

HUMILITY – *A belief that you are not better than others, often characterized as genuine curiosity, gratitude, and a lack of arrogance. A belief that you still have more to learn.*

Confidence Over Competence, Part 1

Entrepreneurs are wired just a bit differently than the rest of the world's population. I've been told that they often have an incredibly high level of optimism, which allows them to believe that anything is possible, and a relatively low level of reality-testing, which allows them to happily pursue opportunities that others would see as risky or downright irresponsible.

As an entrepreneur, I would agree with this. Now that I'm in my 40s, I look back at when I was launching my first team-building company in my 20s and shake my head. I can't believe the unabashed confidence I had to market, sell, and deliver workshops to Fortune 500 companies when I had very little business experience outside of what I had learned in school. Thankfully, at a young age, I was able to quickly grow the business, hire a team, and start to work with teams of all sizes around the world.

At that time, one of my goals was to move into the world of keynote speaking. I loved being in front of a crowd and felt I was quite talented in that space. I just needed to find the right opportunity to make it happen. In my late 20s, I was convinced that this opportunity had presented itself. I was asked by a large corporate event association to speak to their members, a crowd of about 250 people.

I had not done any keynote speaking at that point, but I was delivering workshops to corporate groups every week, so I was confident I would be rock solid as a speaker. I also knew that the largest speaking agency in the country was a member of this association, so their team would get to see me in action at this event. If I played my cards right (which I was confident I would), they would then want to represent me as my agent and my career as a successful keynote speaker would be launched.

I was so confident in this plan, I contacted the speaking agency, introduced myself, and told them to watch for me speaking at the event. I asked if they would be open to chatting with me the week following the event to explore collaborative opportunities, and to my excitement, they agreed.

The event came and I delivered my first keynote. Although I didn't feel amazing about it, I was quite confident it was good enough to clear the path for many more opportunities. The week following the event, I had my call with the VP of the speaking agency. To my shock and discouragement, however, the call didn't go as planned. In a concise and polite way, she was clear that they did not see me as a fit with their agency. When I probed into why this might be, the VP offered two key reasons: lack of helpful content to offer the audience and a lack of skill as a speaker.

I was dumbfounded. How could I be so naïve and my reality-testing be so off? Was this a clear sign that keynote speaking was not for me and I should just "stay in my lane" of delivering workshops? Knowing that I would be running into team members from this speaking agency at future events, should I just avoid them and try to minimize any further embarrassment? Was it time to give up on my dream of keynote speaking?

STEP 1: UNDERSTAND

Most people think that, as a leader, you must choose: You *either* take a "never let them see you sweat" approach and lead with clarity and confidence, *or* you choose the path of humility and lead in a modest and vulnerable way. Successful leaders, however, know that choosing one approach to the neglect of the other will always backfire, and instead, they lead with *both* confidence *and* humility.

Strengths-based Versus Growth Mindset

I'll never forget the epiphany I had 20 years ago when I saw Marcus Buckingham give a keynote on his book, *First, Break All the Rules.*[1] Based on the research project he had just completed—the largest study ever conducted around engagement by the Gallup Organization—it became clear that if I was going to be truly effective in life, I needed to stop trying to fix my weaknesses

> *"Focusing on strengths is the surest way to greater job satisfaction, team performance, and organizational excellence."*
>
> MARCUS BUCKINGHAM

and instead focus my time and energy on leveraging my strengths and natural talents.

This affirmed my decision to be an entrepreneur and become a corporate speaker and facilitator. My strategy in life was to move closer to my unique sweet spot every year so that I could have the biggest possible impact. This meant finding ways to do less of what I wasn't good at (things that weakened me) and do more of what I was uniquely great at (things that strengthened me).

Then, about 10 years after my Buckingham experience, I started to have an annoying but persistent voice in my head that was telling me to sell my business and take on the director role for a 40-bed homeless shelter. But why? This made no sense from a strength's perspective. I didn't have a ton of talent running a shelter, and as much as I had a passion to serve the homeless community, I wasn't too passionate about the roles and responsibilities associated with the director role.

This was also around the time I started to dig into the research of renowned psychologist Dr. Carol Dweck and her work around embracing a growth mindset.[2] Dweck suggested that a passion for stretching oneself, even (or especially) when things were not going well, was the hallmark of true lifelong learning and growth. This meant that I should seek out opportunities to develop new skills, take on hard challenges, and make lots of mistakes.

I ended up listening to the voice in my head, and for close to a decade, I put myself in challenges that were well over my head.

I deliberately moved out of my strengths sweet spot, in the hopes of developing new strengths in an area of work I felt called to do.

Confidence AND Humility

So, who is right? Should I side with Marcus Buckingham and confidently live out my strengths? Or should I follow the teaching of Carol Dweck and humbly embrace a growth mindset?

"Love challenges, be intrigued by mistakes, enjoy effort, and keep on learning... Challenges are exciting rather than threatening. So rather than thinking, oh, I'm going to reveal my weaknesses, you say, wow, here's a chance to grow."

CAROL DWECK

The answer is...YES!

In my life, I've realized that the dilemma between being strengths based and embracing a growth mindset is not a problem to solve but rather a tension to manage. And it points to what I believe is the most important tension you can manage as a leader—being *both* confident *and* humble.

In the 10 years that I operated my first leadership development company, and in the last four years that I've been running Leaders for Leaders, I have been firmly operating out of my strengths every day. As a speaker and facilitator, I am able to leverage my natural talents and work with confidence and expertise, and as a result, I love my job and am able to help leaders and teams thrive.

At the same time, when I look back at my 10 years directing the homeless shelter, I was often a million miles away from confidently living out my strengths. I was humbled every day by what I didn't know and had to learn, and I was forced to continually embrace a growth mindset. This meant learning new skills in areas where I wasn't strong and being OK with making lots of mistakes. And in those years, I tapped into and developed parts of myself that I didn't even know existed. I was able to make a real and significant impact on the world around me.

If there is one secret to great leadership, it is to be *both* fully confident *and* fully humble. When you are able to *both* live out your strengths *and* embrace a growth mindset, you tap into the power of the healthy tension required for success!

Healthy Tension?

By now, it should be clear that finding healthy tension between confidence and humility is critical to resilience and results. As the graphic below illustrates, there are aspects of effectiveness, engagement, and leadership that come from *both* confidence *and* humility; and there are inevitable negative results if you overdo one value to the neglect of the other.

TENSION

Building Confidence and Remaining Humble

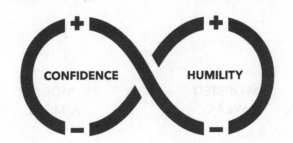

POSITIVE RESULTS OF CONFIDENCE ✚

- Your knowledge and experience leads to expertise
- You are able to inspire and motivate others
- You feel positive and self-assured

✚ **POSITIVE RESULTS OF HUMILITY**

- You are constantly open to learning and growing
- Your vulnerability and modesty make you approachable
- You have a sense of gratitude and curiosity

CONFIDENCE ∞ **HUMILITY**

NEGATIVE RESULTS WHEN OVERDONE ─

- You become ignorant and unwilling to learn
- You come across as arrogant and inflexible
- You feel better and smarter than those around you

─ **NEGATIVE RESULTS WHEN OVERDONE**

- You never fully live out your strengths or true potential
- Others lose out because you're holding back
- You feel inferior and insecure

STEP 2: ASSESS

Reflect on your thoughts and actions this past season. Have you had the confidence to feel self-assured, inspire others, and make a real difference? Have you had the humility and genuine curiosity that allowed you to learn and grow? Take a look at the following graphic and assess which of the four quadrants you are currently living in.

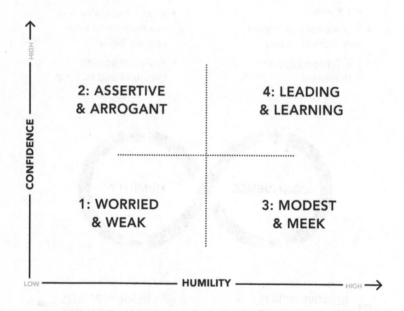

STEP 3: LEVERAGE

Regardless of what quadrant you currently find yourself in, the goal is to spend more and more time in quadrant four. The good news is that there are practical things you can do to gain the positive results of both confidence and humility so you can be *both* successfully leading *and* constantly learning.

Honing Humility

In her book, *Mindset: The New Psychology of Success*, Dr. Carol Dweck encourages you to reflect on a few key questions to determine if you are embracing humility and working with a growth mindset or if you are working with a fixed mindset and potentially being close-minded.

> *"Everyone I meet is my superior in some way, and in that, I can learn from them."*
>
> EMERSON

1. Do you feel threatened by the success of others (fixed mindset)? Or are you inspired by the success of others (growth mindset)?

2. Do you easily give up and move on when facing hard challenges (fixed mindset)? Or do you persevere and work through hard challenges (growth mindset)?

3. Are you primarily focused on performance and how others perceive you (fixed mindset)? Or are you more concerned with learning and getting better (growth mindset)?

4. Do you receive feedback defensively and avoid it (fixed mindset)? Or do you receive feedback as a gift and seek it out (growth mindset)?

5. Do you hate making mistakes and avoid them at all costs (fixed mindset)? Or are you comfortable with making mistakes and see them as a learning opportunity (growth mindset)?

When I was first introduced to these questions and answered them honestly, I was quite surprised at how often I leaned toward a fixed mindset. The educational system I was raised in expected me to always get the right answer—not embrace mistakes! My natural competitive spirit had me struggling to celebrate the successes of others—especially people who were competing against me. And as much as I liked the idea of receiving feedback as a gift, my default reaction was often one of being hurt and becoming defensive.

I also found that both age and success were potentially working against me. The older I got, the more fixed I could become about how I believed things should be done and less open to the opinions and perspectives of others (especially people younger and less experienced than me). The more success I experienced in my work and with my ideas, the less open I could become around accepting failure or making mistakes, and the more focused I could become on maintaining my image and reputation rather than learning and growing. All of this added up to the realization that embracing a growth mindset and being humble is often a lot harder to do than one would expect.

It is important to recognize that everyone has a fixed mindset at times. In fact, there are days where I look back and realize that I've oscillated between fixed and growth a number of times throughout the day. The good news is that embracing a growth mindset is a choice. What I try to do is recognize days, weeks, and seasons when I need to push myself to embrace a growth mindset and then work hard to hang out there as much as possible.

For example, early into the first few months of COVID-19, I had to remind myself over and over that I needed to work hard to embrace a growth mindset, that the challenge of losing a lot of business unexpectedly could provide me with great learning and business innovation opportunities, that the inevitable mistakes I would make transitioning from in-person to virtual delivery were a sign I was being courageous and taking important risks. Embracing a growth mindset and grounding yourself in humility can be challenging, but it is a choice, and it is always worth the effort.

Cultivating Confidence

As I dug deeper into the work of Marcus Buckingham and his research with the Gallup Organization, I realized that I needed to challenge a generally accepted leadership myth: If you work hard and put in the effort, you can do whatever you want in life.

As great and motivating as this sounds, it's simply not true. For example, in my early teens, I could have practised my singing skills 24 hours a day and still wouldn't have secured a spot in the school choir, much less have become a pop sensation. Why? Because I'm a horrible singer. At best, with endless practice and coaching, I might have learned to hold a tune, but I never would have become great. A brutal fact of reality is we all have strengths and weaknesses.

Buckingham went further to stress that if we are going to be fully engaged in life and grow in healthy confidence, the trick is to stop being obsessed with fixing our weaknesses and instead to focus on leveraging our strengths. Rather than spending your time and energy on making something you're bad at become something you're competent at, choose instead to devote your time and energy on making something you're already good at become something you're truly great at.

When you challenge the leadership assumption that you can do anything, accept your weaknesses, and concentrate on developing and unleashing your strengths, you will tap into a healthy and powerful level of confidence.

In her book, *A Return to Love*,[3] author Marianne Williamson offers a powerful and convincing perspective on your responsibility to be confident and bring your strengths to the world:

> "Our deepest fear is not that we are inadequate. Our deepest fear is that we are powerful beyond measure. It is our light, not our darkness that most frightens us. We ask ourselves, 'Who am I to be brilliant, gorgeous, talented, fabulous?' Actually, who are you not to be? You are a child of God. Your playing small does not serve the world. There is nothing enlightened about shrinking so that other people won't feel insecure around you.

> "We are all meant to shine, as children do. We were born to make manifest the glory of God that is within us. It's not just in some of us; it's in everyone. And as we let our own light shine, we unconsciously give other people permission to do the same. As we are liberated from our own fear, our presence automatically liberates others."

I hope her words inspire you to let your leadership shine brightly to those around you.

AND LEADERSHIP IN ACTION
Marnie McBean

Not long ago, a client contacted me wanting me to deliver a leadership development workshop in partnership with Marnie McBean. The client believed that my message around healthy tension and Marnie's message around the power of more would be a perfect complement to one another.

It was true! By the end of our first collaborative call, it became clear that our individual work would be even better together.

The other thing that struck me was that Marnie exemplified the blend of confidence and humility in a powerful way. I knew that she would be the perfect person to interview for this chapter and was delighted when she agreed to contribute.

Marnie is one of Canada's most decorated Olympians, having won three gold medals in the sport of rowing. She is a member of Canada's Sports Hall of Fame and has been made an Officer of the Order of Canada. As a former specialist in Olympic Athlete Preparation and Mentoring for the Canadian Olympic Committee (COC), Marnie prepared athletes emotionally and psychologically to ensure that they performed at the highest level.

In recognition of her work, she was named Canada's Chef de Mission for the 2020 Tokyo Olympics. In this role, she acted as a spokesperson for Team Canada and a mentor for the athletes, coaches, and staff, all with the aim of creating an inclusive environment conducive to optimal performance.

She is also the author of *The Power of More: How Small Steps Help Us Achieve Big Goals*,[4] which outlines how she sets and achieves goals, both in sports and in life.

Action Steps

What are things you can do to gain the positive results of humility?

- **Crave critical feedback.** As an athlete, if my coach spent an hour watching me row and didn't provide critical feedback on how I could improve, I'd be upset. To be the best, you need constant constructive criticism. I needed to know each day what I could be working on to improve from the day before. When I left full-time competition and entered "the civilian world," I realized how rare ongoing feedback was. People would wait until a scheduled performance review to tell me about a concern they had with me months ago. A clear sign that you're not demanding enough feedback is when you go from expecting and craving it to worrying about it and taking it personally.

- **Love to learn.** The reason I stayed in rowing for so many years was because I knew there was so much left for me to learn. I knew I had so far to go in terms of physical strength and technical training. When I started out, I was told that there were 185 things you could do wrong in each rowing stroke (which sounded like a lot), but as I progressed, I realized that number was way too low!

  To be truly great at something is like going down a corridor of doors. You enter a corridor for the first time and think that there are 10 doors to open revealing all you need to know. The amazing thing is, once you have opened those 10 doors, you realize that each door opens a new corridor of 10 doors. When I talk with high-performance athletes about career longevity, I always tell them that they're in the right place to continue if they are still truly curious and excited to open more doors.

What are things you can do to gain the positive results of confidence?

- **Have a "done" list.** Ambitious people are often fixated on their to-do list, but part of confidence is having a "done" list. Staying connected to your successes and being reminded of the challenging tasks you have accomplished helps you deal with the inevitable stress that comes from the desire to achieve great things. Constantly adding to and reviewing your done list will build your confidence as you continue to push forward and through your increasingly busy and challenging to-do list.

- **Find your performance state.** A performance state in sport is when all the physical, mental, and technical elements of your performance perfectly fit together. The balance of these elements is different for every athlete I've worked with.

  I remember working with a world-class diver who was told by coaches and sport psychologists that she was being too hard on herself before competing and needed to integrate positive imagery and positive self-talk during her upcoming Olympic competition. She took this advice and had the worst Olympic experience of her career. After that, she determined that she would never again allow someone else to tell her what her performance state should or shouldn't be. Being confident wasn't what worked for her; she thrived on being worried. That state kept her focused on the details of her performance.

Some of us need encouragement. Some of us need critical feedback. Some of us need quiet time to focus and visualize. Some of us need teammates around us and music blasting in our ears. You have to find what works for you in order to have the confidence/ performance state to win on competition day.

Red Flags

What are early warning signs that you're overfocusing on humility to the neglect of confidence?

- **Not Trusting Your Gut** – I've never been a person to keep my internal dialogue to myself. I generally say what I think and feel. Because of this, anytime I notice myself holding back or supporting a decision I'm not feeling great about, I see that as a red flag. It's not always bad for me to hold back—sometimes it's showing discretion, which is a good thing—but most of the time, it's a sign that I'm not standing in the confidence I should have.

This past year, I have been at the decision-making table to determine how Canada will (or won't) participate in the Tokyo Olympics based on the risk of COVID-19. At times, I found myself holding back or not challenging suggestions I disagreed with because I was listening too much to the voice in my head saying, "Who am I to have an opinion?" That's when I reminded myself that I needed to be brave and have the confidence to offer my opinion and my unique point of view regardless of the outcome.

What are early warning signs that you're overfocusing on confidence to the neglect of humility?

- **Lack of Curiosity** – This can happen on a few levels. Anytime you feel that you've learned enough in your area of expertise and have "opened all the doors" required, that's a red flag. You'll never progress to the level of a champion, veteran, or mentor with a belief that you've learned enough. Instead, you'll inevitably get stuck, and the doors that you have opened will become outdated.

  On an interpersonal level, anytime I find that my conversations are too much about me, what I know, and what I've done, as opposed to what I'm learning or what I can learn from the person, I see that as a red flag as well. I can be guilty of this one! After a conversation with friends, if my wife asks me, "So how's that person doing?," and I don't really know, I take it as a reminder that I have to keep working on this!

Confidence Over Competence, Part 2

After my keynote catastrophe, I decided to put my speaking aspirations on the shelf and simply focus on delivering workshops. However, as the years passed, I was not able to shake the fact that I wanted to be a speaker and that I could be effective and helpful in such a role.

I decided to embrace a long-term plan to live out this dream. In the short term, I would focus on gaining useful experience, which turned out to be a decade of research and writing around the concept of healthy tension and years of practical experience directing the homeless shelter. I would also become devoted to learning as much as possible in the world of keynote speaking. This resulted in taking courses, pursuing countless unpaid speaking opportunities to gain practice, and closely following speakers I admired to learn from the best.

A decade after my keynote went so wrong, I was asked to speak at a large national human resource conference. I knew the same speaking agency that turned me down years ago would be at this event as well. Part of me wanted to reach out to them and ask if they'd be open to seeing me in action one more time. Part of me, however, was terrified to do this, fearing it would result in more rejection and embarrassment.

I decided to set my fears aside, and after reaching out to them, I was amazed that the CEO of the agency quickly responded to say that they would try to take in my keynote. The morning of the event as I was preparing in the meeting room, I noticed the CEO was in a seat in the very back row. I was incredibly nervous but gave it everything I had. Ten minutes before the keynote was complete, I noticed the CEO quietly got up and left the room. I assumed that he had once again decided I was not what they were looking for.

The next day the phone rang, and it was him. He told me that I was exactly what they were looking for at the agency, and they'd like to get a plan in motion right away to start representing me as a keynote speaker!

In the years since that call, I have been blessed with an incredible partnership with this agency that has allowed me to speak to audiences all over the world. The journey that started out with me placing confidence over competence and neglecting humility has revealed the importance and power of tapping into a healthy tension between *both* confidence *and* humility.

ADDITIONAL RESOURCES

- Book – *First, Break All the Rules: What the World's Greatest Managers Do Differently* by Marcus Buckingham and Curt Coffman

- Book – *Mindset: The New Psychology of Success* by Carol S. Dweck, Ph.D.

CHAPTER 9

"UNCOMMON" SENSE LEADERSHIP

Curiosity, Connection, and Courage

We are living in an increasingly polarized world. Every day, whether you're watching the news, scrolling through social media, or talking with your neighbours, you'll find division between people, politics, and perspectives. Liberal versus conservative. Environment versus economy. Unions versus management. Black Lives Matter versus All Lives Matter. What's interesting is that no matter which side people find themselves on, they tend to associate their position with simple common sense.

It's becoming incredibly rare to find leaders who can build bridges that unify instead of walls that divide. How can you stand out from the crowd and take an "uncommon" sense approach that moves people beyond polarization and points them toward a better way? What does it take to lead with AND?

Fundamental Flaw, Part 1

I am one of the fortunate ones in this world who was raised in a stable and loving home. I have a deep sense of gratitude to both my mother and father for putting their all into the responsibility of parenting. That said, I had a very fundamentalist upbringing. A fundamentalist is a person who decides whether something fits within his belief system before he fully explores it.

In our family, our belief system, which was directly connected to our religion, dictated that we did certain things and didn't do other things (a long list of other things, in fact). We believed certain things to be true, which meant that anything else by default must be false. It also meant that a person's beliefs and actions dictated whether they were a good person or a bad person. It was all quite clear cut. Black and white.

For a good portion of my childhood, I never questioned this belief system and code of conduct. In fact, I felt quite safe and secure in it. I assumed that I was better off than most children because I was being raised with such clarity and exposed to such truth.

It wasn't until my early teenage years that I started to question things. Up until then, giving a note to the teacher that excused me from school dances, not listening to any "worldly" music, not playing cards, or not going to movie theatres seemed perfectly normal. But as I thought more and more about these things, I started to realize that I was potentially missing out on something: harmless fun. It was becoming clear and unsettling to me that something about our black-and-white approach to life was flawed.

In my season of soul searching and questioning, I came across this passage by St. Teresa of Avila, and the words stopped me in my tracks:

> "If we choose to live a more spiritual life, then we need
> to become more spontaneous, more engaged, and more

contemplative. Living a spiritual life means we are able to live our life in total polarity.

"This means we are at ease in the in-between spaces:

Between traditional *and* progressive viewpoints
Between rational *and* emotional responses
Between taking action *and* just being there
Between solitude *and* leisure
Between fasting *and* feast
Between discipline *and* wildness.

"If we are not growing in our spiritual life, then we get stuck on one end of the spectrum or the other, and we can end up bland, lukewarm, mediocre, and isolated. The only way to live a spiritual life is to be able to touch both sides at the same time. Knowing that it is in the interplay between living the spectrum (of these opposite polar forces) that we deepen our spirituality and become more aware of who we are, whom we choose to be, and in challenging times how we show up."

These words strongly resonated with me, and even though the passage was written over 500 years ago, it provided relevant and timely language for the thoughts and ideas that I was processing at the time. I knew that when the author talked of a "spiritual" life, she wasn't talking about religion; she was talking about living an "in-spirited" life—living life with energy, vitality, and to its fullest.

This was how I wanted to live! I had realized the limitations and harm that overdone Either/Or thinking had caused and was ready to embrace an AND approach to life.

But this meant I had to face a significant dilemma. If I was going to make this change and see the world through less of a black-or-white, right-or-wrong perspective, I had to be prepared that some would see me as a heretic. I'd seen this happen time after time with others who shared our fundamentalist approach to life but had decided not to conform with the rules of the belief system. I'd be an outsider. I'd be judged. I'd potentially be alone.

Was the benefit of pursuing a new approach to life that aligned with my evolving values and beliefs worth the cost of what I'd inevitably lose in the process?

STEP 1: UNDERSTAND

The Three Cs

Today, finding uncommon sense leaders can be challenging; however, when you do, you'll discover that they always possess three unique characteristics: curiosity, connection, and courage. Understanding these characteristics and exploring how you can embrace them is a guaranteed way to take your leadership to the next level.

Staying Curious

Curiosity is the desire to learn about and understand things. It's about being inquisitive, and it's based on the assumption that you're always missing something. If you want to see this in action, hang around children.

My wife is a grade one teacher, and during COVID-19, I had the privilege of listening in on some of her virtual lessons. It was amazing! It didn't matter what she was teaching, the children were mesmerized by every topic and full of endless questions.

I listened in on a class that focused on healthy food choices and a balanced diet, and the children's questions made me laugh out loud: If jellybeans are beans, does that mean they are a vegetable? If you eat more good foods, can you eat more bad foods? If bad foods hurt your body, why don't they arrest the people who make them? The questions went on and on until Becky was out of time.

Curiosity results in learning, growing, and embracing every opportunity that life presents. Sadly, as the years pass, our curiosity often diminishes. If you peek into the average high school class, you'll quickly realize that things have changed quite a bit from the grade one scenario I just described. You'll often find teenagers that are indifferent and uninterested. Their curiosity has been replaced with concern—concern for things such as what notifications they're missing on their phone or how they're measuring up to the expectations of their peers.

Now think of the average workplace. What matters most in that environment is being "right" and aligning with others on the team who share your "correct" point of view. People have clear views on how they should serve the client, how the business should be run, and how the team should be aligned. Close-mindedness and overconfidence have killed curiosity.

In his book, *Think Again*,[1] thought leader Adam Grant offers three indicators that you've lost your spirit of curiosity: You're known for preaching, prosecuting, or politicking. "When we become so wrapped up in preaching that we're right, prosecuting others who are wrong, and politicking for support, we don't bother to rethink our own views and get trapped in an overconfident cycle," Grant said.

Think about this from a political perspective. Chances are you lean a bit toward the left and embrace a liberal bias, or you find yourself leaning toward the right and embracing more conservative values. Does this result in any preaching, prosecuting, or politicking?

As the preacher, you feel the need to come off as 100% certain of your values and beliefs in order to be persuasive and hopefully convert others. This creates a false sense of security and leaves you vulnerable to dismissing facts and data that impact you. When you think of your recent political conversations, have you tended to take the role of the preacher?

As the prosecutor, your goal is to attack the other side's "case" in order to discredit and defeat it. This approach refuses to acknowledge any wisdom or value in the opposite point of view, which results in your inability to expand or improve your own position. It also results in divisive and polarized relationships. When discussing a policy from the opposite political side to yours, do you take the prosecutor role, attacking and discrediting the policy without being curious about the possible benefit it's aimed at achieving?

As the politician, your goal is to be accepted. As a result, you adopt popular opinions to get "votes." The value you place on being liked outweighs your desire to understand what you truly believe or to be curious about other points of view. When you think of your political views, how many of them are shaped by the acceptance and approval of those around you? How comfortable would you be to openly support policies and beliefs that you know your close friends and family disagree with?

Beyond the common tendency to become a preacher, prosecutor, or politician, something else threatens our curiosity. By the time we are adults, our brains have developed a cognitive bias, or an error in our thinking, called a confirmation bias.

A confirmation bias simply means that you will seek out information, interpret situations, and recall data to affirm your beliefs and points of view. This means that if you lean toward the right in the U.S., you're more likely to watch Fox News, and if you lean toward the left, you're more likely to watch MSNBC or CNN. It also means that if you lean to the right and a left-leaning government is in power, you will find and focus on lots of examples of the government's failings; yet, if you lean to the left, you'll be focusing on and celebrating all the examples of the government's success. Interestingly enough, both perspectives will be valid; however, they'll both be incomplete.

In my first book, *The Power of Healthy Tension*,[2] I suggest what I believe to be the single most powerful way to reclaim your natural curiosity and overcome the tendency to be close-minded and overconfident: Embrace your opposite. This means that you are consciously at war with your confirmation bias, and instead of seeking out information to affirm your beliefs, you're searching for information that

> *"Learn something new from each person you meet. Everyone knows more than you about something. Ask people what they've been rethinking lately or start a conversation about times you've changed your mind in the past year."*
>
> ADAM GRANT

challenges them. Instead of being a preacher, prosecutor, or politician, you strive to be a pupil, a student of life who is constantly open to learning new things and embracing new and diverse perspectives. Embracing your opposite means that you're deliberate about talking to people, listening to news sources, and looking for data that comes from the opposite point of view to yours.

What's important to understand is that embracing your opposite and "staying curious" is not about switching sides and exchanging your values and beliefs for someone else's; it's about expanding your values and beliefs to consider someone else's so that you grow in wisdom, understanding, and leadership effectiveness.

Seeking Connection

Celeste Headlee is an award-winning journalist, author, and speaker. In her 2015 TED Talk, "10 Ways to Have a Better Conversation,"[3] which has now been viewed over 24 million times, she explains how our world is becoming more and more divided.

In the talk, Headlee describes, "[a] world in which every conversation has the potential to devolve into an argument, where our politicians can't speak to one another, and even the most trivial issues have someone fighting both for it and against it." Her argument is based on a Pure Research study of 10,000 American adults that demonstrates we are more polarized and disconnected than we ever have been in living history. She adds that because of this, people are also less likely to compromise or acknowledge common ground. Our world is divided!

Uncommon sense leaders are connectors. By leading with AND, they find ways to connect ideas and viewpoints that others assume are incompatible. They foster authentic connection with diverse people whose views and beliefs are often different from their own. And they are often a relational catalyst, connecting people and unifying teams that otherwise would be divided and polarized by differences of opinion. In a world that is increasingly building walls of division, uncommon sense leaders stand out for building bridges of connection.

The best way to seek connection is to develop and practise the skill of empathy. This is the ability to see where another person is coming from and understand her values and fears. Empathizing with people who are like you and who gen-

We are more polarized and disconnected than we ever have been in living history.

erally share your points of view isn't too hard for most people. Empathizing with people who are different than you and have values and beliefs contrary to yours is a lot more challenging.

Author and empathy expert Lee Hartley Carter calls this rare form of the skill "active empathy."[4] She stresses that it's important to remember that to actively empathize with people does *not* mean you have to agree with them; however, she adds, you *do* need to be open-minded enough to see the world from their perspective.

There are three common assumptions we make about people who have different biases and viewpoints than ours that block our ability to empathize and stop us from seeking connection:

a) We assume they are less informed (or even less intelligent) than we are.

b) We assume that they care less about the situation than we do.

c) We assume that they are not as "good" (i.e., have inferior morals, values, etc.) as we are.

Let's go back to our right wing/left wing political example. If you lean toward the right and have a conservative bias, it would be easy for you to assume the following about people who lean to the left:

a) They don't really understand what works and what doesn't work when it comes to the economy and social policy like you do.
b) They don't seem to care about values like freedom, independence, or prosperity as much as you do.
c) They don't care about family values or freedom of religion as much as you do.

And if you lean to the left, the specific words might be different, but the underlying assumptions toward people on the right would likely be the same.

What does it look like to completely turn those assumptions around? This means that your default assumptions towards all people, especially people with different beliefs and biases than you, are as follows:

a) They have wisdom they can share with you.
b) They care about the situation as much as (or more than) you do.
c) They are every bit as "good" as you are.

When you start to embrace these assumptions, you unleash the power of active empathy, and inevitably, you become a connector. The calluses and blinders that were created from over-focusing on differences start to come off, and your eyes and heart are opened to see the good in all people and the wisdom in diverse opinions. Because of this, you extend the gift of unconditional acceptance to people, regardless of your acceptance or agreement with their values or beliefs.

And they know it! They feel it! As a result, they are likely to feel a connection with you and be equally open to your diverse viewpoints as well.

Showing Courage

Courage is having the mental and moral strength to face danger, pain, or difficulty head on. When we're young, we identify the heroes in the movies we watch, history books we read, and sports we follow as those who possess a high degree of courage.

As adults, when we see courage displayed in others, such as in the front-line workers who are currently fighting COVID-19 day in and day out, we hail them as heroes. As parents, courage is one of the core values that my wife and I have tried to develop in our two children since they were infants. It's a value that most people admire and aspire to live out, yet it's something we often fail to demonstrate when it matters.

I do my best to live without regret, framing things from my past that I would change or was embarrassed by as opportunities to learn and grow. That said, there are a few things that still bother me.

Becoming a leader who has the ability to hold conflicting values in tension and to embrace Both/And thinking takes courage.

One of the few regrets I still have is my failure to be courageous in grade nine. This was the year I left my small country elementary school to attend a big city high school. I desperately wanted to fit in and be accepted but unfortunately was far from being part of the "in" crowd.

My best friend from elementary school was even more unpopular than me. For some reason, right from the first week of high school, the "cool" kids singled him out as a target and horribly bullied him. Although it bothered me that they bullied my friend, there was also a part of me that was somewhat relieved the focus was on him and not me.

Throughout the year, there were numerous times I was with my friend when he was being verbally or physically bullied, yet I did nothing. I always tried to console him afterwards, but I never had the courage to stand up for him while the bullying was happening.

Many years later, I went to him and asked for his forgiveness for my lack of courage and support. He generously forgave me and told me it wasn't a big deal. But it was a big deal! Instead of showing the value of courage, I let the reality of fear win the day—fear of standing out from the crowd, fear of being unpopular or ostracised, and fear of not having the strength that was required to stand up to bullies.

Becoming a leader who has the ability to hold conflicting values in tension and to embrace Both/And thinking takes courage. It means that you must move beyond the safety and support that comes from picking sides and being part of a tribe. It means that you must move beyond the confidence and ease you feel from believing you're right all the time. It means that you must at times disappoint, frustrate, and challenge people in your life that you value and want to accept you. It means you must face your fears.

The amazing thing is that once you do face the fears that hold you back from being courageous, your world starts to move from black and white to full colour. Not only do you gain the ability to see things from a fresh and fuller perspective, your self-esteem and self-regard begin to grow as you become truly proud of yourself and the strength you have. Something else amazing happens as well: your courage liberates courage in others. But we'll talk more about that in the final chapter.

STEP 2: ASSESS

Moving from an Either/Or to a Both/And approach to leadership takes a high level of curiosity, connection, and courage. Do you have what it takes on all three scales to lead with AND?

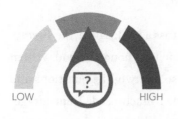

CURIOSITY

- Constant desire to learn and understand new perspectives
- Assumes you are always missing something
- Inquisitive and open

CONNECTION

- Finds common ground between polarizing viewpoints
- Develops authentic relationships with people who see the world differently
- Builds bridges instead of walls

COURAGE

- Moves beyond the comfort of picking sides
- Desires challenge and push-backs on their views and beliefs
- Can support views and beliefs that disappoint or frustrate others

STEP 3: LEVERAGE

AND LEADERSHIP IN ACTION
Greg Paul

When I was approximately two months into my job leading the homeless shelter, I started to question if I had bitten off more than I could chew. I was becoming overwhelmed by the pressure of the expectations I didn't believe I could deliver on and the heaviness of the life-or-death situations we were dealing with every single day. I started to wonder anxiously if I had made a terrible mistake in taking on this new role.

Then, by providence, I came across a book called *The Twenty-Piece Shuffle*[5] by author Greg Paul. It felt as though he had written the book just for me. He addressed so many of the questions and struggles I was having and provided much-needed encouragement and perspective. I was so impacted by the book that I sent an email to Greg to thank him for his work. To my surprise, a few days later, he emailed me back, and that led to an unexpected friendship and mentorship that proved to be life changing for me.

Greg Paul is a pastor and member of Sanctuary in Toronto, a ministry where the wealthy and poor share their experiences and resources daily to care for the most excluded people in the city, including addicts, prostitutes, homeless people, and street-involved Indigenous and LGTBQA2+ folks. A father of four and husband to Maggie, he is also the author of *Queer Prophets, Close Enough to Hear God Breathe, The Twenty-Piece Shuffle,* and *God in the Alley.*

Talk about when you came to the realization that you needed to move beyond Either/Or thinking?

I was brought up with a fundamentalist outlook on life. Not only were things *either* right *or* wrong, there were also clear outcomes a person should expect when they did these wrong or right things. This meant that if you believed and did the right things, your life should work out just fine.

This approach to life began to break down for me when I started hanging out with marginalized people. I quickly realized that the street-involved people we were walking with who often had experienced addiction and significant trauma didn't always get the results I expected from believing and doing the "right" things. In fact, they rarely did. I recognized a disconnect between what I believed to be true and reality, which was proving that this "truth" wasn't working. The key was understanding that this wasn't because of the failure of other people or failure in me, it was a flaw in my thinking and understanding.

For a while, I took a somewhat irrational approach to life where I was becoming more and more convinced that my Either/Or, right/wrong approach wasn't working, yet I still pursued it. A time came, however, when I had to decide if I was going to cling to an approach that didn't work in the real world and was constantly leaving me frustrated, or if I was going to begin to dismantle my beliefs.

I chose to dismantle.

Moving forward, I would use whether an idea actually *worked* to help me determine if the idea was true or not.

Share your thoughts around the need to stay curious.

Curiosity is so critical. It's not, "I changed my mind, and now this is true." Instead, it's a continual process of letting go of your assumptions and refining your thinking. Being truly curious allows you to free yourself from the traps of your own ego and accept that you're not in control. This doesn't mean you're throwing out your belief system; it simply means you're opening your hands with your ideas, knowing some may leave and some may stay. And if some stay, then they might even be truer than you thought.

Share your thoughts around the need to seek connection.

Language is a powerful thing. It's important to recognize that the more you learn to hold things in tension, the more your language will shift as well. However, the language of the people you came from and who still provide a significant portion of your resources and influence will probably not change.

This means that if you want to maintain connection with your tribe and influence them in a positive way, you need to think about how you communicate with that group. There's a place for shock and pushing the boundaries, but ultimately, your goal is to communicate effectively. You'll find that you can express what you mean without shocking or terrifying people because of divisive language.

Share your thoughts around the need to show courage.

It's terrifying to hit a point when the assumptions on which you've built your life begin to erode. It takes courage to ask yourself the question, "Do I want to stay in an environment where my ideas don't work and are polarizing people?" It's even scarier when you realize that it's not as easy as letting go of one thing and grabbing onto something else; it's letting go and not knowing where you're going next. That's a frightening moment!

But once you discover the fortress you built to protect yourself has actually become a prison that is keeping you from growing, you'll see the value of leaving it behind. Breaking free is an act of faith, regardless of your belief in God.

Why do you believe that leading with AND is so important in our world today?

We are living in a world filled with fundamentalists, and I'm not only talking about religion. It's politics as well. Liberals and conservatives both believe that there is a code, and if you don't fully believe in and align with this code, you're evil and contributing to some form of "hell." It's often just the conservatives who get criticized for this, but it's not difficult to find people on the left who are just as bad.

The same is true with people's polarizing views around the economy, and the same is true with people's views on sociology. We are living in a culture of limited, binary thinking. It's this or it's that. We desperately need people who have the courage to rise above this destructive approach to life and build unifying bridges instead of divisive walls.

Fundamental Flaw, Part 2

It's time to go back to the I decision I had to make in the opening story: Could I move beyond a clearly flawed black-and-white, Either/Or approach and start to embrace an AND approach to life? If so, was I able to accept being seen as a heretic and a disappointment to the friends, family, and community that I cared about?

What was incredibly helpful to me at that time was challenging my understanding of what it meant to be a heretic. I had assumed this basically meant that you were a lost soul who chose to run away from what was good and true.

It turned out I was wrong! I recognized that a heretic was actually a person who embraced the tension between his belief system and something different, wrestled with it, and then decided whether to accept the new idea or reject it. In other words, a heretic was a person with enough courage to resist conforming. This new understanding made me realize that being called a heretic wasn't something to fear or be ashamed of; in fact, it was a badge of honour.

I started to notice something else that was quite profound as well. As I studied movements of social justice and people who had huge impact on the world, I realized that many of these individuals had been called heretics as well. But they still had the courage to lead in a way that challenged the status quo of their core community and held conflicting values in tension instead of choosing sides. Because of this, the people around them—even some of their closest friends and allies—criticized and ostracised them for it.

I researched the work of Dr. Martin Luther King Jr. As the most visible leader in the American civil rights movement, his work earned him the Presidential Medal of Freedom, a Nobel Peace Prize, and a federal U.S. holiday established in his name. Today, people at both ends of political and social continuums share in their support of his beliefs and his methods.

At one time, however, his approach was seen as much more heretical. As he navigated the tension between *both* change *and* stability, he faced criticism for aligning with both sides. On one hand, more militant African American thinkers felt his commitment to nonviolence and relationship building with white political leaders was not drastic enough and failed to demand the change that was required. On the other hand, his vision of racial integration was criticized by other grassroots movements for jeopardizing and devaluing their unique African American culture.

Similarly, when people think of anti-apartheid revolutionist Nelson Mandela, South Africa's first black president, they generally picture him as an icon of social justice and a worthy recipient of the 1993 Nobel Peace Prize. Yet, he lived a life of constant criticism, and he was punished for what were perceived as heretical views.

I had the privilege of travelling to South Africa and going to Robben Island where Mandela served 27 years of imprisonment. As I learned more about his life and his work, it became clear that he had the courage to embrace the tension between *both* having high expectations *and* extending grace. Because of his high expectations, critics on one side attacked him for being a communist terrorist who would be responsible for the ruin of South Africa. Because of his grace, critics on the other side attacked him for being too open to reconciling and negotiating with apartheid's supporters instead of demanding justice.

In 2008, I traveled to Kolkata, India. There I was able to spend time at the headquarters of the Missionaries of Charity, which was home to Mother Teresa and where her body was laid to rest. I was moved to tears as I learned about how she responded to a calling in her life to not only serve the poor, but to live among them. This resulted in over 4,500 nuns in over 120 countries running orphanages, AIDS hospices, and charity centers that cared for refugees, the homeless, and victims of floods, epidemics, and famine. Mother Teresa received the Nobel Peace Prize in 1979, and in 2016 she was officially recognized as a saint.

However, like both Dr. King and Mandela, Mother Teresa was also criticized for her views and strategies. But even when perceived as heretical, she courageously pursued the tension between *both* optimism *and* realism. Her organization unapologetically shared the reality of poverty with the world, but critics attacked her for spreading what they argued was an overly negative view of Kolkata and for promoting of a "cult of suffering."

At the same time, she took every opportunity possible to inspire hope and optimism through stories of the lives saved and changed through her organization. For this, she was criticized for exaggerating the impact of her work and even for being manipulative in order to raise funds.

> *"Change is made by people, by leaders, who are proud to be called heretics because their faith is never in question."*
>
> SETH GODIN[6]

The more I studied the lives of people who had incredible impact on the world, the more it became clear to me that difference-making and being accused of heresy often go hand in hand. But if the title of heretic is a requirement for following in these leaders' footsteps, then I aspire to become a heretic—a curious, connected, and courageous heretic.

ADDITIONAL RESOURCES

- Book – *Think Again: The Power of Knowing What You Don't Know* by Adam Grant

- Book – *The Twenty-Piece Shuffle: Why the Poor and Rich Need Each Other* by Greg Paul

- Video – "10 Ways to Have a Better Conversation," Celeste Headlee, https://www.ted.com/talks

CHAPTER 10

HOW TO STAY IN THE GAME (AND ENJOY THE ADVENTURE)

RESILIENCE – *The ability to recover quickly from difficulties, adversity, or major challenges*

RESULTS – *Desirable or beneficial consequences or effects. A favourable outcome.*

Burnt Out and Bitter

We all have people we look up to. As children, we commonly look up to our parents, professional athletes, rock stars, and celebrities. As we get older, we often add professionals to this list, people who are renowned in the areas of business, social services, education, or government that we are passionate about.

This was certainly the case for me. It started as I launched my first for-profit business and had a list of CEOs and entrepreneurs who I closely followed and deeply admired. It continued when I moved into my role at the homeless shelter and started looking up to certain executive directors and well-known social justice advocates.

To my surprise and delight, my career allowed me the privilege of meeting and sometimes even getting to know some of the very people I looked up to. As a leadership development author and speaker, I have been able to work with some well-known business icons. My work in homelessness has provided me with the opportunity to work with a handful of social justice and social service "celebrities" as well.

You'd think that this would be a dream come true, but in many cases, it turned out to be a massive disappointment. What I found time and time again was that, as I started to get to know the real people "behind the curtain," they turned out to be far from who I expected them to be. Fighting an uphill battle against broken systems, impossible demands, and unreasonable people had made them bitter and on the verge of burnout. They could flash a smile for the camera and give a great interview on demand, but in reality, they were pretty miserable to be around.

> I started to wonder if becoming bitter and burnt out was just a cold, hard reality for anyone who chose the path of leadership.

Similar to discovering the truth about the Tooth Fairy or Santa Claus, this was an incredibly disheartening realization for me. It also provided me with insight into why I would often see high-potential individuals who seemed to be gaining leadership traction and starting to make a difference simply give up and throw in the towel. They must have decided that the price of leadership just wasn't worth it and chose to take an easier road with a brighter horizon. I started to wonder if becoming bitter and burnt out was just a cold, hard reality for anyone who chose the path of leadership.

Thankfully, I have come to realize that this view of leadership was incomplete. I have also gotten to know a short list of inspiring leaders who have successfully blazed a trail down the path less travelled without losing their joy along the way. I now have proof that it *is* possible to lead change and make a difference while holding onto your principles and retaining your peace of mind.

How is this possible? By moving beyond Either/Or thinking and embracing Both/And thinking. By taking an AND approach to leadership.

Unfortunately, too many leaders get weighed down by the shackles of Either/Or thinking, and as a result, they live with the pressure that they must be right all the time. Because of this, despite the best of intentions, they lead in a way that is divisive and polarizing, and they inevitably become burnt out and bitter.

> *"PEACE. It does not mean to be in a place where there is no noise, trouble, or hard work. It means to be in the midst of those things and still be calm in your heart."*
> UNKNOWN

Successful leaders rise above this all-too-common approach and learn to hold conflicting values in tension. They replace the word "or" with the word "and." They move from win-lose to win-win. They build bridges instead of walls.

As a result, they lead with a sense of peace that comes from not having to be right all the time. They lead with a sense of hope because they know that resistance and opposition often come from a good and wise place. They lead with a sense of optimism because they understand that even the most polarizing and divisive points of view are commonly aligned around a shared higher purpose. They have found a way to stay in the game *and* enjoy the adventure.

AND LEADERSHIP IN ACTION
Bonnie Wesorick

Bonnie Wesorick is a healthcare transformation legend! After a 20-year nursing career that earned her the reputation of someone who shook things up in hospital rooms and emergency departments, she went on to work with hundreds of healthcare organizations and thousands of interprofessional providers across the continent to create the best places to give and receive care.

To honour and expand the legacy of her work, The Bonnie Wesorick Center for Healthcare Transformation has been created at Grand Valley State University, Michigan. Bonnie also serves as a technology adviser to the American Academy of Nursing.

I met Bonnie many years ago when we were both participating in a small and intimate two-year mastery program that studied the concept of Polarity Management.[1] From the moment I met Bonnie, I knew something was different about her. She had a presence that radiated *both* confidence *and* humility, and she seemed to ooze 100% pure joy.

As the years passed and I grew to understand all the ways that Bonnie has been—and continues to be—a world-changer and difference-maker, I've been fascinated by how she stays in the challenging game of healthcare transformation without getting bitter or burnt out.

To learn more, I asked Bonnie several questions around the secret to her resilience and results. I'm confident you'll find the answers as insightful and challenging as I did.

Resilience

You've been committed to leading people, projects, and organizations in order to transform healthcare for over 40 years now, yet somehow, you haven't become jaded or bitter in the process. What's your secret?

- **Let go of the pressure.** Once you understand that some problems are unsolvable and get comfortable with holding things in tension, you experience an incredible amount of freedom and relief. You no longer need to be right all the time! You no longer feel pressure to get everyone to see things from your point of view; in fact, you're moved to seek out resistance and diverse perspectives. You can freely say, "I don't know, but do you? And can you help me understand?" You lose your defensiveness and stop taking everything personally.

- **Don't waiver!** I started my career with 100% clarity that I wanted to serve people by being a nurse. I have never lost my passion and commitment to serving people, and I have never lost my passion and commitment to being a nurse. I realized early in my career that to have the most impact possible, I would need to take on more leadership responsibility; however, I have always seen myself first and foremost as a nurse. With new roles, responsibilities, and leadership titles, it's easy to wake up one day and realize that, despite all your successes, you've drifted a long way from your true north. The key to staying passionate and positive is not to let that happen.

Results

Your work has had significant impact worldwide in the transformation of healthcare, and you have created a lasting legacy through the businesses you've developed, books you've written, and The Wesorick Center. How have you been able to achieve such incredible results in an area known for bureaucracy and broken systems?

- **Embrace Both/And thinking.** When I left the "ideal world" of nursing school and started to work in the "real world" at the hospital, I began to see the same troubling thing over and over again: I was surrounded by a brilliant and caring team of people who were spending most of their waking hours at work exhausted, frustrated, and hopeless. Something was clearly not right!

  As I tried to understand why this was, I began to notice something interesting. Every time our team faced a challenge, we would assume it was simply a problem to solve, and our job was to pick the *right* answer or choose the *right* side. I started to realize that this was a flaw in our thinking! The challenges we faced were rarely situations that required Either/ Or thinking, but instead, they required Both/And thinking. It's been said that a moment of insight is sometimes worth a life's experience, and for me, this insight changed everything.

By narrowing down the ongoing challenges we were facing, and replacing "or" with "and," we were able to take strong positive action and sustain it:

- It wasn't medical care *or* whole person care; it was medical care *and* whole person care.

- It wasn't patient safety *or* staff safety; it was patient safety *and* staff safety.

- It wasn't cost of service *or* quality of service; it was cost of service *and* quality of service.

Suddenly, through the power of Both/And thinking, we realized that change *was* possible. And working in a challenging environment like healthcare didn't have to be exhausting, frustrating, and hopeless.

- **Pass it on!** Once I started to move beyond problem solving and embrace Both/And thinking, I just kept saying to myself, "Holy smokes, this is a gift!" And when you receive a gift, the best thing you can do is share it. Then, the question became, "Who should I share it with?"

I wholeheartedly believed (and still believe) in the wise words of author Parker Palmer[2] who defines a leader as "a person who has an unusual degree of power to project on other people his or her shadow or his or her light...[and] conditions which can be illuminating and uplifting to the people or conditions which can cast them into total darkness."

Because of this belief, I became fanatical about bringing the power of Both/And thinking to leaders within healthcare. I realized that if we could help develop leaders and then hold them accountable, they'd have the highest potential to unite people and create positive change. Once a leader truly grasps the power of AND, they understand that a healthy culture is one where diverse people are connected, and an unhealthy culture is one where people are divided regardless how brilliant or dedicated they are.

Lead the Way

I never have been and never will be known for my athletic abilities or my accomplishments in competitive sports. I was the kid who tried out for most of the teams in high school but always got cut. As a result, I learned to embrace sports like fishing and hiking, activities where my chances of getting "cut" were minimal.

That said, one competitive sport I started to dabble in when I was in my 20s was running. It began when a friend of mine, who happened to be a Canadian champion in long-distance running, told me that regardless of my lack of hand-eye coordination or ball-handling skills, if I put the work in and trained properly, I could successfully run a 5K race within a few months.

He was right! And to my surprise, running turned out to be something that I quite enjoyed. My 5K turned into a series of 10Ks, and then in the year I turned 30, I ran my first half marathon. Despite the Kenyan who passed me while running a *full marathon*, I had succeeded! (OK, it bothered me a little, but I was still feeling great.)

Now it was time to set a big, hairy, audacious goal. Not only was I going to run a full marathon, I was going to run the New York City Marathon. This 26.2-mile race through the streets of New York City draws over 50,000 participants, making it the largest marathon in the world.

To achieve this goal, however, I had a few big challenges in front of me. Beyond the training and preparation required, the New York City Marathon is also one of the hardest marathons to get into. To compete, you have to enter your name into a lottery and the odds of getting selected are around 16% to 18%. I applied in 2008 and was denied. Then I applied again in 2009, 2010, and 2011. Denied! Finally, in 2012, something amazing happened—I got in. It happened. This was my year!

After approximately six months of training, I was ready to head to New York, but in the week leading up to the race, a real problem started to emerge. An Atlantic tropical storm had developed into a full-blown hurricane, *and* it was headed straight for New York. Hurricane Sandy turned out to be the strongest, deadliest, and most destructive storm of the 2012 hurricane season. It caused at least 182 deaths in the U.S. and resulted in over $60 billion in property damage. It had ravaged New York City.

In the days leading up to the race, there was a ton of uncertainly about whether it would be cancelled or not. New York City Mayor Michael Bloomberg vowed that the race would go ahead, saying that New York needed something to be excited about and something that would demonstrate the city's resilience and ability to bounce back.

Based on this, I boarded a plane and headed to New York. The plane was practically full of runners who, like me, were all wondering if their decision to run the race was a wise one. During the flight, I started to notice a lot of conversations between passengers and what seemed to be a growing feeling of concern and disbelief. It turned out that by watching the news on the airplane TV sets, they had just learned that Mayor Bloomberg had changed his mind and decided to cancel the marathon less than 48 hours before it was due to start.

As soon as I touched down at the airport, I was hard at work trying to get back to Canada. This was much easier said than done, as I was one of thousands trying to depart the city. After approximately 24 hours of what felt like an episode of *The Amazing Race*, I made it home. I was exhausted. I was disheartened. And I was also heavy-hearted for the people of New York.

In the planes, trains, and automobiles required to get me out of the city, I gained an on-the-ground look at the impact of the hurricane. It was devastating. I had never seen anything like it, and I started to feel a sense of guilt and shame for being so concerned about the loss of my race when people all around me were dealing with the loss of their homes and loved ones.

When I arrived home and was preparing for a much-needed sleep after being up for what seemed like a lifetime, my phone rang. A wonderful and caring friend called to tell me she saw what had happened with the cancellation of the marathon. Knowing how much work I had put into preparing, she generously offered to fly me to another city in the U.S. where another marathon was taking place the very next day.

After thinking about it, I countered the offer. I told her that I would run the 26.2 miles the next day on the trail system close to my house, and instead of buying me the plane ticket, she could donate the money to the American Red Cross' campaign set up to help support people in New York devastated by the hurricane. She agreed, and the plan was set.

Just before turning off the light and hitting the pillow, I decided to do an update on Facebook, letting my friends know I was home safe and sound, and I had a new plan to run a local race to help raise funds. I noted that they too could donate to the cause. After that, I went to sleep—for about 18 hours straight!

The next morning when I woke up, I quickly noticed that my phone had completely blown up while I was sleeping with countless notifications and voicemails. To my amazement, I found that for the first (and only) time in my life, I had gone viral. The Facebook post had spread beyond my circles of connections, and people were commenting and—more importantly—donating from across the world. I had newspapers waiting to get in touch with me to cover the story, and tons of friends were reaching out to ask if they could run parts of the race with me. I was in utter shock and disbelief.

When I arrived at the starting point of the makeshift race, I was blown away once again. There was a crowd! The gathering was made up of not only people I knew, but people I had never met before. Runners from far and wide were lacing up their shoes and doing their pre-race stretches, as they too had decided to run the race to raise funds. It was absolutely incredible.

Four hours later when I finished the race, there were banners, cheering crowds, and TV news anchors waiting to interview me. More importantly, I found out that thousands upon thousands of dollars had been raised to help those hit hard in New York, and the money was still coming in.

In the days to follow, upon reflection, I had somewhat of an epiphany: "Most people want to make a difference and help

> *Most people want to make a difference and help to make the world a better place; they just don't know where to start. They need someone to lead the way.*

to make the world a better place; they just don't know where to start. They need someone to lead the way."

To this day, almost a decade later, I keep in touch with several people who ran the marathon with me in 2012. For some, it awakened within them a passion for difference-making, and they continue to run races for charity each year. They just needed someone to clear the path, and then they were unstoppable.

I've now seen this phenomenon lived out in many ways over the past 10 years. I have witnessed many people show up to the doors of the homeless shelter and say to me, "I have no idea where to start or what I can do, but if there's any way I can help, I'm in!" Then I would watch as these same people would go on to be some of our most incredible volunteers, impacting the lives of the marginalized and excluded in life-changing ways.

I'd talk to farmers who would thank me for giving them the opportunity to donate their fruit to our jam company social enterprise. They had tapped into the sense of significance that they longed to feel; they just needed someone to clear the path and show them where to start.

A Time to Lead

Most of this book has focused on how leading with AND is the one skill you need to succeed as a leader, how learning to hold things in tension is the best way to ensure you avoid becoming bitter and burnt out and instead gain resilience and achieve results. I am excited for you to experience this for yourself and to see your leadership break through to the next level of effectiveness.

As I conclude, I want to challenge you to go beyond focusing on the personal gains you'll achieve by leading with AND and focus on how you can lead the way for others. I encourage you to consider how, by modeling and teaching Both/And thinking to those around you—your teams, your colleagues, your friends, and your family—you will clear the path for them to lead with AND as well.

Our world is becoming more and more polarized and divided. The need to be right, pick sides, and vilify those on the other side is destroying our quality of life and the health of our relationships. And everyone knows it!

We can see how broken our political systems are becoming. We have all experienced the anxiety and fear that can arise when we sense someone has a polarized bias or point of view different from ours. We see and feel the impact of division all around us and want things to be better. Most of us just don't know how to be part of the solution, and even if we did, we're scared to take a first step. We need people to help us safely move beyond the divisiveness of Either/Or thinking and learn instead to lead with AND.

In the first chapter, I took some time to define and unpack my definition of a leader: a person who is responsible for moving things forward and driven to make a difference. Now is your time to lead. You're responsible as a leader to display the curiosity, courage, and connection others need to see in order to follow you down the adventurous path of holding things in tension. Others need to see the positive difference you make in the world as your Both/And approach builds bridges instead of walls. They need your leadership to give them the courage and confidence to start to think, work, and relate differently.

Our world, our organizations, our communities, and our families are reeling from mistakenly treating every issue as if it is *either* right *or* wrong, good *or* bad, win *or* lose. But there's hope! Leaders like you are showing the watching world around them that there is a better way and another path to take, that tension is actually a good thing and the best road to experiencing the win-win outcomes they long for. All that is required is to move beyond the traps of Either/Or thinking and have the courage to lead with AND.

FREE RESOURCE

To thank you for purchasing this book, I want to provide you with a free resource that will allow you to create a personal action plan around key concepts and big ideas.

Simply visit www.leadwithand.com and download the Personal Action Plan. This digital journal includes chapter summaries, tension maps, and assessment grids, as well as space for you to create a plan you can immediately put into action.

WWW.LEADWITHAND.COM

NEXT STEPS

For further growth opportunities, check out
these easy and effective ways to help your entire
organization learn to lead with AND:

KEYNOTES – One-hour presentations that motivate
and inspire your audience to reach higher and dig
deeper. Virtual and in-person options available.

WORKSHOPS – Insightful and engaging virtual
and in-person programs that boost morale, develop
leadership, and align teams to thrive.

ONLINE COURSE – A self-directed, five-module
course that will help you thrive in a world of
complexity and polarization. Includes teaching videos,
editable workbook, and reflection activities.

SIMPLY VISIT **WWW.TIMARNOLD.CA** TO LEARN MORE.

NOTES

CHAPTER 1

1. https://bcorporation.net/

2. https://www.compassionatestc.ca/

CHAPTER 2

1. Jann S. Wenner, "Obama in Command: The Rolling Stone Interview," *Rolling Stone,* October 2010.

2. Tim Arnold, *The Power of Healthy Tension: Overcoming Chronic Issues and Conflicting Values* (Amherst, MA: HRD Press, 2017).

3. Barry Johnson, *Polarity Management: Identifying and Managing Unsolvable Problems* (Amherst, MA: HRD Press, 1992).

CHAPTER 3

1. Jim Collins, *Good to Great* (London, England: Random House Business Books, 2001).

2. Daniel Goleman, *Emotional Intelligence: Why It Can Matter More Than IQ* (New York, NY: Bantam Books, 1995).

3. Daniel Goleman, "What Makes a Leader?," *Harvard Business Review,* November–December 1988.

4. https://www.reuvenbaron.org/wp/
   description-of-the-eq-i-eq-
   360-and-eq-iyv/

5. Stephen Covey, *The 7 Habits of Highly Effective People: Restoring the Character Ethic* (New York, NY: Simon & Schuster, 1989).

6. Based on the Polarity Map® and Principles of Barry Johnson and Polarity Partnerships LLC.

7. Kim Scott, *Radical Candor: How to Get What You Want by Saying What You Mean* (London, England: Pan Books, 2019).

8. Based on the Polarity Map® and Principles of Barry Johnson and Polarity Partnerships LLC.

CHAPTER 4

1. Elisabeth Kübler-Ross, *On Death and Dying* (New York, NY: Macmillan Publishing Company, 1969).

2. Andrew Grove, *Only the Paranoid Survive: How to Exploit the Crisis Points That Challenge Every Company and Career* (New York, NY: Currency Doubleday, 1996).

CHAPTER 5

1. Simon Sinek, *Start with Why: How Great Leaders Inspire Everyone to Take Action* (New York, NY: Penguin Books, 2011).

2. Greg McKeown, *Essentialism: The Disciplined Pursuit of Less* (New York, NY: Crown Business, 2014).

3. Bureau of Labor Statistics' Business Employment Dynamics, 2017.

4. Gallup, *State of the Global Workplace,* 2017.

CHAPTER 6

1. Brené Brown, *Dare to Lead: Brave Work. Tough Conversation. Whole Hearts* (London, England: Vermilion, 2018).

2. Janice Fenn, *Chandra Goforth Irvin, Do You See What I See?: A Diversity Tale for Retaining People of Color* (San Francisco, CA: Pfeiffer, 2005).

3. Cari Jackson, *The Gift to Listen, the Courage to Hear* (Minneapolis, MN: Augsburg Books, 2003).

4. https://indigenousfoundations.arts.ubc.ca/ sixties_scoop/

CHAPTER 7

1. Daniel Goleman, *Social Intelligence: The New Science of Human Relationships* (New York, NY: Bantam Books, 2006).

2. https://blog.marketresearch.com/the-10-billion-self-improvement-market-adjusts-to-new-generation

3. Stephen Covey, *The 7 Habits of Highly Effective People: Restoring the Character Ethic* (New York, NY: Simon & Schuster, 1989).

4. http://www.lauralizhughes.com/

5. https://invisiblechildren.com

6. Daniel James Ladinsky, *Love Poems from God: Twelve Sacred Voices from the East and West* (New York, NY: Penguin Compass, 2002).

7. Henry Cloud, John S. Townsend, *Boundaries: When to Say Yes, How to Say No to Take Control of Your Life* (Grand Rapids, MI: Zondervan, 1992).

CHAPTER 8

1. Marcus Buckingham, Curt Coffman, *First, Break All the Rules: What the World's Greatest Managers Do Differently* (New York, NY: Simon & Schuster, 1999).

2. Carol S. Dweck, *Mindset: The New Psychology of Success* (New York, NY: Random House, 2006).

3. Marianne Williamson, *A Return to Love* (New York, NY: HarperCollins, 1996).

4. Marnie McBean, *The Power of More: How Small Steps Help Us Achieve Big Goals* (Vancouver, British Columbia: Greystone Books, 2012).

CHAPTER 9

1. Adam Grant, *Think Again: The Power of Knowing What You Don't Know* (New York, NY: Viking, 2021).

2. Tim Arnold, *The Power of Healthy Tension: Overcoming Chronic Issues and Conflicting Values* (Amherst, MA: HRD Press, 2017).

3. www.ted.com/talks/celeste_headlee_10_ways_to_have_a_better_conversation

4. Lee Hartley Carter, *Persuasion: Convincing Others When Facts Don't Seem to Matter* (New York, NY: TarcherPerigee, 2020).

5. Greg Paul, *The Twenty-Piece Shuffle: Why the Poor and Rich Need Each Other* (Colorado Springs, CO: David C. Cook Publishing, 2008).

6. Seth Godin, *Tribes: We Need You to Lead Us* (New York, NY: Penguin Group, 2008).

CHAPTER 10

1. Barry Johnson, *Polarity Management: Identifying and Managing Unsolvable Problems* (Amherst, MA: HRD Press, 1992).

2. Parker Palmer, *Let Your Life Speak: Listening for the Voice of Vocation* (San Francisco, CA: Jossey-Bass, 2000).

ACKNOWLEDGMENTS

I want to start by expressing an incredible amount of gratitude to my wife, Becky, and two kids, Declan and Avryl. Not only did this book mean that I had to spend many Saturday mornings writing in my office instead of hanging out with them, they also had to put up with me rambling on about *Lead with AND* way too much over the past few years. Their love and support—and the tensions we are learning to manage together—made this project possible.

The vision for this project was strongly tied to securing interviews from amazing leaders who I felt managed the six leadership tensions better than anyone I know. When I made my wish list of the leaders I wanted to interview, I prepared myself for rejection, knowing they all were incredibly busy and in high demand. To my amazement, everyone I reached out to graciously said yes.

Tim Masson, Mary Ann Schlabach, Walter Sendzik, Allison Alley, Donald Miller, Tim Schurrer, Colin McAllister, Justin Ryan, Chandra Irvin, Jason Russell, Marnie McBean, Greg Paul, and Bonnie Wesorick, I can't thank you enough. Your insights and practical suggestions took this book to the next level.

Thanks to the amazing team of friends and professionals who provided editing, creativity, and overall direction to this book throughout the entire writing process. Claudia Valle, Ally Fallon, Annie Kyle, Scott Russell Dempster, Christa Hesselink, Rachel Krause, and Cathy Williams, I am so blessed to have you in my corner.

And finally, I thank God for the amazing opportunities that have come my way and the incredible connections I have been able to make. These have combined to make this project possible, and for that (and so much more), I am truly blessed beyond measure.

ABOUT THE AUTHOR

Tim Arnold has spent over two decades helping leaders manage complexity, increase resilience, and deliver results within organizations such as the United Nations, Compassion International, Royal Bank of Canada, Allstate Insurance, Toyota, and Siemens.

After running both a for-profit business and a homeless shelter, Tim leverages his real-world experience to help organizations pursue both profit and purpose. His work focuses on helping leaders unleash the superpower of Both/And thinking in an Either/Or world.

Beyond leadership and team development, Tim is an avid fisherman, world traveller, and really bad hockey player. His biggest accomplishments are being dad to Declan and Avryl, and husband to Becky.

WWW.TIMARNOLD.CA